CLAUDIA ALLEMEERSCH

THE OVEN COOKBOOK

For AGA and other top cookers

Lannoo

Content

My AGA and I...	9
Recipes for...	10

Appetizers 13
Cauliflower snacks 14
Camembert fondue 15
Crostini with avocado 16
Snails with herb butter 17
Scones with cheese, olives and onion 19
Soufflé with green herbs 21

Soup 23
Potato soup with rosemary crackers 24
Bisque d'homard 27
Pea soup with smoked sausage 28
Chicken cream soup with leek 29
Minestrone 30
Fish soup with pastis 33

Pasta & rice 35
Lasagne with salmon and fennel 38
Lasagne quattro formaggi 39
Pumpkin lasagna 40
Pasta with merguez 43
Pasta shells with kale and artichoke 44
Champagne risotto with ricotta 47
Frittata with cauliflower 49

Potatoes 51
Potato pie 52
Oven fries with chilli mayonnaise 53
Potatoes with fungi, sage and bacon 54
Potato gratin 55
Potatoes with tomato crust 57
Potato dish with mozzarella 58
Fondant potatoes 59
Gratinated potato puree with sausages 60
Roast potatoes 61
Roast sweet potatoes with chicken 62
Hasselback potatoes with bay leaves 65
Duchesse potatoes with parsnips 66
Buttermilk stampers 67
Parmentier with shrimps 68

Veggie 71
Butternut with kale stuffing 72
Bean dish 74
Burrata with roasted aubergine 75
Mushroom strudel with spinach 77
Cottage pie 78
Roasted cauliflower 79
Roasted pumpkin 80
Kohlrabi gratin 81
Mexican vegetable dish 82
Leek rolls 84
Radicchio with ricotta 85

Pizza 87
Pizza with ceps and quail egg 88
Basic dough for pizza 88
Pizza with broccoli and spinach 89
Pizza raclette 91
Pizza pancetta 91

Traybake 93
Tray bake with young carrots and chipolatas ... 94
Tray bake with chicken and paprika 95
Tray bake with salmon, carrot and bok choy 96
Tray bake with sweet potato,
fennel and ricotta 99

Fish 103
Dorade with ratatouille and pesto 104
Glazed cod 105
Lobster scarmoza 106
Mussels with leek 109
Smoked sardines 110
Lobster with green herbs 111
Plaice with red endive 112
Plaice with clams 113
Redfish with tomato and asparagus 114
Sole à la dugléré 115
Haddock rarebit with white cabbage and kale .. 116
Lemon sole with turmeric 119
Fish waterzooi 120
Sea bass with aioli 123
Sole hollandaise 124
Wolffish with curry 125

Meat & poultry ... 127

- Canard à l'orange ... 128
- Cassoulet ... 131
- Coq au vin ... 132
- Pigeon with peas ... 135
- Roast pheasant ... 136
- Glazed duck ... 139
- Stuffed pheasant ... 140
- Guinea fowl with morels ... 143
- Spring chickens with wild mushroom cream sauce ... 144
- Pheasant stew ... 146
- Crusty vol-au-vent ... 147
- Swedish meatballs ... 149
- Boeuf bourguignon ... 152
- Roasted veal crown ... 155
- Blanquette of veal ... 156
- Ossobuco ... 159
- Leg of lamb with figs ... 160
- Saddle of lamb with herb crust ... 161
- Lamb daube ... 163
- Moussaka ... 165
- Slow-cooked leg of lamb with mint ... 166
- Meatballs with pumpkin and oyster mushrooms ... 168
- Minced bread with hidden eggs ... 170
- Roast belly pork ... 171
- Glazed belly ribs ... 173
- Italian minced meat dish ... 174
- Stuffed cauliflower ... 175
- Paté with pistachios ... 176
- Meatloaf ... 178
- Sausage rolls ... 179
- Belgian endive dish with minced meat ... 181
- Hare paté ... 182
- Rabbit as mum makes it ... 185
- Hare stew ... 186
- Young venison ragout ... 189

Desserts ... 191

- Meringue with fresh cranberries ... 192
- Crème caramel ... 195
- Gingerbread crumble with apple and pear ... 196
- Red fruit with quark ... 197

Pastry ... 199

- Apple strudel ... 200
- Almond cake with pear ... 202
- Amaretti ... 203
- Applesauce tart ... 204
- Biscuit rose ... 205
- Apple pie ... 206
- Blueberry cake ... 208
- Brownies ... 209
- Chocolate-tipped meringue sticks (billygoat hoofs) ... 210
- Cocoa biscuits ... 212
- Chocolate cake with hazelnut ... 213
- Chocolate bars ... 214
- Frangipane cake ... 215
- Lemon sand cake ... 217
- Dundee cake ... 218
- Chocolate cookie with hazelnut ... 220
- Honey biscuits ... 221
- Cherry flan ... 222
- Cinnamon sprites ... 224
- Christmas cake ... 225
- Almond snaps ('chatterboxes') ... 226
- Coconut bar ... 227
- Misérable ... 228
- Nut cake with salted caramel ... 231
- Coconut rocks ... 232
- Gingerbread ... 233
- Pear tart with almonds ... 234
- Quatre-quarts cake ... 235
- Quatre-quarts apple cake ... 236
- Quatre-quartsgingerbread-apple cake ... 236
- Rice tart with coconut ... 239
- Rice tart express ... 240
- Fast bread pudding ... 241
- Orange tart with liqueur ... 242
- Tartine russe ... 245

Bread **247**
　Banana bread..248
　Breakfast pistolets....................................249
　Brioche oven dish with dulce de leche 250
　Pesto roll 253
　Grape bread..254
　Flatbread with avocado spread................257
　Luxury bread with sweet cinnamon filling 258
　Morrocan bread 260
　Nut rolls.. 261
　Pear and roquefort bread.........................263
　Sugar loaf...264
　Za'atar rolls 265

Katrien Callewaert **268**
　Basic tomato sauce...................................269
　Involtini di pesce......................................270
　Turkey ossobuco 273
　Pasta pomodoro with lobster in basil butter 275
　Radiatori al 4 formaggi 276
　Spaghetti with sage butter 279
　Tagliatelle with ricotta and pancetta 280

Dries Cloet **282**
　Celery gratin Anne-Marie........................283
　Farm chicken crapaudine 285
　Meat and vegetable confetti 286
　Mussels thermidor 289
　Oven dish à la Delphine Parmentier 290
　Cheese and bacon pizza 293
　Lamb tagine...294
　"Marieke's cups"- yoghurt tart..................297

Ellen Dulst **298**
　Pear frangipane..299
　Cod boulangère.. 300
　Chicken balls in Flanders fields 303
　Spring chickens Brabançonne................. 304
　Mediterranean meat loaf.........................307

Eddy Noppe **308**
　Basic recipe puff pastry............................ 309
　Burned pear tart.......................................310
　Cheese biscuits 313
　Kilometre tart with fresh fruit..................314
　Toasts with smoked salmon pralines 319

AGA: love at first sight!..............................**321**
　Blinis 322
　Bread tulips..324
　English breakfast.....................................325
　Egg fried on the simmering plate 327
　Merguez, mushrooms and tomatoes in
　the baking oven..328
　Bacon on the grill plate in
　the roasting oven.....................................328
　White beans in tomato sauce in
　the roasting oven.....................................329
　Toast in the toaster on the boiling plate 329
　Dried chillies 330
　Dried orange slices..................................330
　Vegetable chips...331
　Herb pancakes..332
　Orange, mango and
　passion fruit marmalade 333
　Marmalade cake 334
　Mussels...336
　Mussels with fine spices...........................337
　Naan flatbread..338
　Pancakes...339
　Popcorn 340
　Salmon wraps...341

Recipe index..344
Ingredient index..348

Superb oven dishes

My AGA and I...

are a passionate story in themselves, which I would like to tell you more about later in this book. Added to that, I really like to use an oven for cooking anyway. For me, the preparation of oven dishes is synonymous with pure and intense flavours, fragrant aromas, conviviality and a slightly slower way of cooking, which I personally really appreciate. Baking, braising, roasting or slow cooking... just about all the different ways you can use an oven are covered in the book. In addition, I give the preparation methods for both a regular type of oven and for the AGA. So there is something for everyone, both in terms of technology and taste. The dishes have been carefully selected to serve both complete, indulgent meals and to quickly magic a fragrant casserole onto the table on a busy weekday. I sincerely wish you and your family and friends richly atmospheric moments at a table with delicious dishes.

All recipes in this book have been written for a conventional oven with top and bottom radiant heat. It is best to bake in the middle of the oven.

If, however, you are using a convection oven, you may need to adjust the temperatures given in the recipes. The forced circulation of hot air means that the heat is transferred more quickly, allowing you to cook faster than in a normal oven. A disadvantage is that that this can sometimes be a bit too fast and burn your dish. We therefore recommend that you set the temperature slightly lower and cover the oven dishes with baking paper. An advantage is that you can bake on several levels in the oven.

A handy rule of thumb when choosing the temperature:

Conventional °C	Hot air °C
50	45
100	90
125	110
150	135
160	145
175	155
180	160
190	170
200	180
225	200
240	215

The baking time can also be reduced a bit, but everyone knows their own oven best!

The instructions for an AGA cooker are also included and the following terms are used for this: here we use the names of the different ovens as a guide and not the temperature.

In each oven too, the temperature varies. The higher, the warmer. For example, to grill a dish, place it as high as possible in the roasting oven, where the hottest temperature is. With the latest AGA electric cookers, the temperature is more evenly distributed in each oven.
Cook in the ovens as much as possible.
Keep the hob lids closed as much as possible.
Place all oven dishes on a rack, except for bread and pizza. These can be baked directly on the oven floor.
Because you cannot see inside the ovens, a side dish can sometimes be forgotten, with all the consequences. This can be remedied by placing a magnet on the doors behind which dishes are being prepared.
Always bring soups, stews and liquids to the boil on the hob before placing them in the cooking or simmering oven.
Stews require at least 3 hours in the simmering oven.

Get to know your oven and check that the indicated temperature is correct. How far does the temperature drop when you open the oven door? How long does it take for the oven to heat up again? All these details can have a major impact on your baking result. Our stated temperatures and baking times are a guide, but please adjust them to your own oven.

Liquid measures			Oven temperatures	
Metric	Imperial	Us	°C	°F
25ml	1fl oz		110	225
50ml	2fl oz	¼ cup	120	250
75ml	3fl oz		140	275
100ml	3½fl oz		150	300
120ml	4fl oz	½ cup	160	325
150ml	5fl oz		180	350
175ml	6fl oz	¾ cup	190	375
200ml	7fl oz		200	400
250ml	8fl oz	1 cup	220	425
300ml	10fl oz/½ pint	1¼ cups	230	450
400ml	14fl oz		240	475
450ml	15fl oz	2 cups/1 pint		
600ml	1 pint	2½ cups		
750ml	1¼ pints			
900ml	1½ pints			
1 litre	1¾ pints	1 quart		

BOILING PLATES	Boiling plate	Left hand hob	400 °C
		Large enough for 3 saucepans	
		Strong heat	
		Boiling water	
		Stir-frying	
		Toasting bread	
		Searing meat	
	Simmering plate	Right hand hob	250 °C
		Large enough for 3 saucepans	
		Gentler heat	
		Making sauces	
		Heating milk	
OVENS	Roasting oven	Baking meat	240 to 260 °C
		Grilling at the top of the roasting oven	
		Baking bread	
		Roasting poultry	
	Baking oven	Baking bread, cakes and biscuits	180 to 200 °C
		Cooking fish and poultry	
		Lasagnes	
	Simmering oven or slow cooking oven	Slow stewing and simmering	120 °C
		Stews and ragouts	
	Slow cooking oven	Boiling, steaming and simmering	90 to 100 °C
		Stocks	
		Stews and ragouts	
		Soups	
		Curries	
	Warming oven	Keeping prepared food warm	70 to 100 °C
		Plate warming oven	

Weights for dry ingredients

20g	¾ oz	300g	11oz
25g	1 oz	350g	12oz
40g	1½oz	400g	14oz
50g	2oz	450g	1lb
60g	2½oz	500g	1lb 2oz
75g	3oz	550g	1¼lb
100g	3½oz	600g	1lb 5oz
125g	4oz	650g	1lb 7oz
150g	5oz	700g	1lb 9oz
175g	6oz	750g	1lb 11oz
200g	7oz	800g	1¾lb
225g	8oz	900g	2lb
250g	9oz	1kg	2¼lb

APPETIZERS

Appetizers that immediately set the tone

Appetizers are the first thing you serve, so I personally like to pay special attention to these. Even with unexpected Fishitors, the oven is your ally in creating simple culinary indulgence. At our home, for example, a Camembert is garnished with fresh herbs and slid into the oven with a dash of whiskey. Ready in the twinkling of an eye, and super delicious! A classic Kurt often asks me to serve and which is always right on target is snails with herb butter.

2 cloves garlic, peeled and shredded
2 tablespoons olive oil
400 g cauliflower rice
100 g cheddar, grated
2 teaspoons dried oregano

1 teaspoon paprika
1 egg white
pepper and salt
300 g pickled grilled red pepper, drained
2 anchovy fillets, drained

40 g nuts of your choice
1 teaspoon capers, drained
1 tablespoon harissa

Cauliflower snacks

Pre-heat the oven to 200 °C.

Briefly sauté 1 garlic clove in the olive oil and add the cauliflower rice. Allows to simmer for 3 minutes and stir regularly. Take the pan from the heat and leave to cool briefly.

Place the cauliflower rice in a large mixing bowl and add the cheddar, oregano, paprika and egg white. Season with pepper and salt and mix well.

Divide the mixture between little buttered baking moulds or ramekins and press well with a spoon.

Bake for 20 minutes in the pre-heated oven until golden brown.

Meanwhile, mix the remaining garlic clove with the other ingredients into a tapenade.

Serve the snacks with the tapenade.

AGA

Bake on the bottom of the baking oven.

TIP

Making cauliflower rice is easy. Grate a cauliflower with a coarse grater or cut the cauliflower into pieces and grind in a food processor into granules.

FOR ONE CAMEMBERT

1 camembert in a wooden box
leaves of 2 sprigs thyme
1 clove garlic, peeled and sliced
dash of whiskey
1 tablespoon honey
pepper and salt

Camembert fondue

Pre-heat the oven to 200 °C.

Remove the paper and foil from the Camembert, return the Camembert to the box and off cut the top rind.

Sprinkle the thyme and garlic over the cheese and press it into the cheese.

Drizzle with a splash of whiskey and the honey. Season with pepper and salt.

Place the camembert on a small oven tray and bake for 10 minutes in the pre-heated oven.

Present the camembert with bread or Belgian endive leaves for dipping.

AGA

Place the camembert box directly on the bottom of the roasting oven.

FOR 1 CIABATTA
1 shallot, peeled and shredded
2 tomatoes, peeled and concentrated
1 tablespoon red wine vinegar
4 tablespoons olive oil
pepper and salt
pulp of 4 avocados
juice of ½ lemon
1 clove garlic, peeled and pressed
250 g ricotta
2 tablespoons finely chopped chives
1 ciabatta loaf
16 basil leaves

Crostini with avocado

Pre-heat the oven to 180 °C.

Mix the shallots, tomatoes, red wine vinegar and olive oil into a vinaigrette. Season with pepper and salt.

Mix the avocado, lemon juice and crushed garlic and mash with a fork.

Add the ricotta and the chives and mix.

Cut the ciabatta into slices and toast for 8 minutes in the oven.

Spread the ciabatta with the avocado and serve with the basil leaves and vinaigrette.

AGA

Toast the ciabatta slices on the left boiling plate.

TO SERVE 2

FOR THE HERB BUTTER:
- 1 shallot, peeled and shredded
- 2 cloves garlic, peeled and pressed
- 2 tablespoons curly parsley, finely chopped
- 1 tablespoon chives, finely chopped
- 250 g butter, at room temperature
- pepper and salt
- 4 drops Tabasco

FOR THE SNAILS
- 12 tinned snails
- 12 shells

Snails with herb butter

HERB BUTTER
Mix all ingredients into a smooth herb butter.

SNAILS
Pre-heat the oven to 175 °C.

Drain the snails well.

Put a snail in each shell and fill with herb butter.

Place the shells in sixes on small fireproof dishes.

Bake for 15 minutes in the pre-heated oven.

Serve with toasted baguette.

AGA

Fry the snails in the top of the baking oven.

FOR 12 SCONES
1 onion, peeled and shredded
1 tablespoon olive oil
175 g self-raising flour
pinch of salt
1 teaspoon mustard powder
1 teaspoon cayenne pepper
½ teaspoon black pepper
25 g butter, at room temperature
1 egg, beaten
6 black olives, pitted and cut in half
55 + 25 g cheddar, grated
1 egg beaten with 30 g milk

Scones with cheese, olives and onion

Pre-heat the oven to 220 °C.

Fry the onion in the olive oil until golden brown. Set aside and leave to cool.

Place the self-raising flour with the salt, mustard powder, cayenne and black pepper in a mixing bowl and mix.

Rub in the butter.

Add the egg, the fried onion, the olives and 55 grams of cheddar cheese and knead into a homogeneous dough.

Roll out the dough to about 2 centimetres thick.

Divide the dough into 5 centimetre squares using a ruler and a sharp knife.

Place a sheet of baking paper or a baking mat on a baking tray and arrange the dough squares on top.

Brush the scones with the egg-milk mixture and sprinkle with the rest of the cheddar.

Bake for 20 minutes in the pre-heated oven.

Leave the scones on a wire rack to cool.

AGA

Fry the onion on the simmering plate.
Bake the scones as high as possible in the roasting oven.

TIP

Replace the onion, olives and cheddar with:

30 g ketchup | 1 clove garlic, peeled and pressed | 1 teaspoon dried oregano | 55 + 25 g Parmesan cheese

150 g sun-dried tomatoes, chopped | 75 g Boursin | 25 g Parmesan cheese

2 spring onions, cut into rings | 1 teaspoon fresh thyme leaves | 1 fresh goat's cheese | 50 g flour

1 shallot, peeled and shredded | 1 pointed pepper, finely chopped | 6 sage leaves, finely chopped | 150 g finely chopped pancetta | 55 + 25 g Parmesan cheese

Sauté the shallot with the pointed pepper and the sage and leave to cool.

Soufflé with green herbs

FOR 20 RAMEKINS

butter and flour for the ramekins
30 g butter
45 g flour
5 dl whole milk
pepper and salt
nutmeg

2 egg yolks
5 dl cream 40%
25 g curly parsley, finely chopped
25 g chervil, finely chopped
25 g finely chopped chives
20 tarragon leaves, finely chopped

125 g Gruyère cheese, finely grated
30 g Parmesan cheese, finely grated
4 egg whites

Pre-heat the oven to 180 °C.

Grease the ramekins with butter and dust with flour.

Melt the butter in a large saucepan and mix in the flour well. Leave the roux to dry. Add the milk while stirring. Bring to the boil and stir vigorously until you get a smooth béchamel sauce. Season with pepper, salt and nutmeg.

Beat the yolks with the cream, remove the pan from the heat and mix the yolks well into the sauce.

Stir the green herbs and the grated cheeses into the sauce.

Beat the egg whites until stiff and fold gently into the mixture.

Distribute between the ramekins, place on an oven tray and bake for 15 minutes in the pre-heated oven.

Serve immediately.

AGA

Make the roux on the simmering plate.
Bake the soufflés in the centre of the baking oven.

SOUP

Soup: a flavour bomb

I'm often asked about the 'secret' of the intense and at the same time pure taste of some of my soup dishes. The answer is simple: I prepare them in advance and then slow cook them in the oven. In this way the flavours have plenty of time to slowly develop. Serve this surprising and intense flavour bomb in a beautiful earthenware bowl and enjoy.

TO SERVE 4

FOR THE CRACKERS:
150 g flour
125 g butter
2 tablespoons chopped rosemary needles
½ teaspoon cayenne pepper
pinch of salt
100 g Parmesan cheese, finely grated
zest of ½ lemon

FOR THE SOUP:
2 sweet white onions, peeled and roughly chopped
2 cloves garlic, peeled and shredded
30 g butter
600 g floury potatoes, peeled, rinsed and cut into equal chunks
2 leeks, cleaned and in rings
pepper and salt
nutmeg
2 sprigs rosemary
1 litre of chicken stock
2 dl cream

Potato soup with rosemary crackers

CRACKERS

Pre-heat the oven to 180 °C.

Put all the ingredients for the crackers into a food processor and knead briefly into a dough.

Roll into a sausage in cling film and place in the freezer for at least 1 hour.

Place a sheet of baking paper or a baking mat on a baking tray.

Cut equal slices from the dough and place them on the baking paper. Make sure they don't touch. The dough is good for about 20 pieces.

Bake in the pre-heated oven for 15 minutes until golden and crispy.

Leave the biscuits on a wire rack to cool.

SOUP

Fry the onion and garlic in the butter in a cast iron pan for 2 minutes.

Add the potatoes and the leeks and allow to simmer for 10 minutes on a medium heat.

Season with salt, pepper and nutmeg and add the sprigs of rosemary.

Add the chicken stock and the cream, cover with the lid and cook for 20 minutes.

Remove the sprigs of rosemary and blend the soup very finely.

If necessary, season further with pepper and salt.

Serve the soup with some rosemary and the crackers.

AGA

Fry the vegetables on the simmering plate.
Bring the soup to the boil, cover with the lid and place in the slow cooking oven for 40 minutes.
Bake the soufflés in the centre of the baking oven.

TO SERVE 4

- 300 g raw lobster shells, chopped
- 50 g olive oil
- 4 shallots, peeled and roughly chopped
- 1 large onion, peeled and roughly chopped
- 3 cloves garlic, peeled and roughly chopped
- 70 g tomato paste
- 150 g cognac
- 1 carrot, cleaned and sliced
- 1 celery stalk, cleaned and roughly chopped
- 4 sprigs tarragon
- 2 bay leaves
- 4 sprigs thyme
- 500 g tomatoes, quartered
- pepper and salt
- 1 litre fresh poultry stock
- 2 dl white wine
- 1 teaspoon cayenne pepper
- 8 saffron threads
- 2 dl cream 40%
- meat of 2 lobsters
- olive oil

Bisque d'homard

Chop the lobster shells into pieces and place in a sturdy mixing bowl. Mash them finer.

Fry the shells in the olive oil on a high heat for about 5 minutes until golden brown.

Add the shallots and the onions and leave to simmer for 3 minutes.

Add the garlic and tomato purée, mix well and flambé with the cognac.

Let the flames go out and loosen the burnt residues in the pan with a spatula.

Add the carrot, celery, tarragon, bay leaf, thyme and tomatoes and season with salt and pepper. Let it simmer for a while.

Deglaze with the poultry stock and white wine, cover with the lid and leave to simmer for 40 minutes.

Remove the tarragon and thyme sprigs and the bay leaves from the soup. Add the cayenne pepper and saffron and mix the soup finely. Strain the soup through a pointed sieve.

Put the strained soup on a low heat and add the cream while stirring.

Fry the lobster meat briefly in olive oil and divide between deep plates.

Pour in the soup and finish with extra pepper.

AGA

Fry the lobster shells and stew with the other ingredients on the boiling plate.
Let the soup simmer, with the lid on, in the slow cooking oven for 60 minutes.
Stir the cream into the soup on the simmering plate.

TIP

Fresh poultry stock is made quickly. Put a chicken in a saucepan of cold water and bring to the boil. Skim off and keep at boiling point for 1½ hours. Strain and clarify.
Add half a roughly chopped fennel for an extra aniseed flavour.
A generous plate of crustacean soup with lobster meat is already a complete dish. Keep this in mind when compiling your menu.
Be careful when using cayenne pepper: rather a little less than too much.

TO SERVE 8

2 onions, peeled and roughly chopped
1 leek, cleaned and in rings
1 celery stalk, cleaned and roughly chopped
2 sprigs thyme
1 bay leaf
1 clove garlic, peeled
50 g butter
700 g frozen peas
4 fresh mint leaves + extra mint to garnish
2 litres poultry stock
pepper and salt
2 tablespoons cream
croutons
2 smoked (dried) sausages, sliced

Pea soup with smoked sausage

Fry the onion, leek, celery, thyme, bay leaf and garlic in the butter for a few minutes and stir briefly.

Add the peas and the mint and deglaze with the poultry stock. Season with pepper and salt.

Bring the soup to the boil and leave to simmer for 20 minutes.

Mix the soup and strain through a pointed sieve. If necessary, season with pepper and salt. Add the cream and mix.

Spoon the soup into plates or bowls and finish with the croutons, extra mint leaves and slices of smoked sausage.

AGA

Fry the vegetables on the simmering plate. Bring the soup to the boil, cover with the lid and place in the slow cooking oven for 30 minutes.

TO SERVE 4

FOR THE POULTRY BOUILLON:
1 Malines chicken
2 cloves
2 onions, peeled and halved
2 carrots, peeled and roughly chopped
2 celery stalks, cleaned and roughly chopped
2 leek stalks, cleaned and roughly chopped
2 cloves garlic, peeled
10 peppercorns
4 sprigs thyme
4 stalks parsley
2 bay leaves
2 dl white wine

FOR THE SOUP:
115 g butter
75 g flour
pepper and salt
2 egg yolks
2 dl cream 40%
dash of sherry

FOR THE GARNISH:
2 leeks, cleaned and in julienne
30 g butter
pepper
2 sprigs thyme

Chicken cream soup with leek

POULTRY BOUILLON
Place the Malines chicken in a large saucepan, just cover with water and bring to the boil. Skim off.

Prick the cloves into a piece of onion. Add the onion along with the other ingredients and bring to the boil.

Let the bouillon draw for about 3 hours on a very low heat.

Remove the chicken from the bouillon, allow it to cool and cut it into pieces. Reserve.

Pour the bouillon through a straining cloth.

SOUP
Melt the butter in a large saucepan and mix in the flour well. Leave the roux to dry. Add the strained bouillon, stirring all the time. Bring strongly to the boil and stir vigorously until you get a smooth soup. Season with pepper and salt.

Put the egg yolks into a bowl and beat them with the cream to form a liaison.

Remove the soup from the heat and stir in the liaison until the soup gets a nice shine. Add a dash of sherry for taste. Keep the soup hot but don't let it boil again.

Sauté the julienne of onions in the butter and season with pepper.

Remove the thyme leaves from the sprigs.

Divide the chicken between the bowls or deep plates, pour over the soup and finish with the leek and thyme leaves.

AGA

Bring the chicken to the boil on the boiling plate. Have the bouillon draw for about 3 hours in the simmering oven.
Make the soup on the boiling plate.

TIP

You can replace the Malines chicken with any type of poultry.

Minestrone

TO SERVE 4

- 1 red onion, peeled and shredded
- 25 g olive oil
- 200 g frozen peas
- 100 g Borlotti beans
- 100 g green broad beans
- 1 celery stalk, cleaned and diced (brunoise)
- 100 g courgette, diced
- 1 leek, cleaned and diced
- 100 g pumpkin, peeled and diced
- 1 carrot, cleaned and diced
- 100 g white cabbage, cleaned and diced
- 2 tomatoes, peeled, seeded and diced
- 1 broccoli, cleaned and cut into small florets
- 10 basil leaves
- 2 sprigs thyme
- 1 litre poultry stock
- 1 tablespoon tomato paste
- 400 g tomato passata
- handful small pasta
- pepper and salt
- 2 tablespoons finely chopped chives
- 50 g Parmesan cheese, grated

Sauté the onion in the olive oil.

Add the peas, beans, celery, courgette, leek, pumpkin, carrot, white cabbage, tomatoes, broccoli, basil and thyme.

Moisten with the poultry bouillon and add the tomato paste and passata.

Simmer with the lid on for 20 minutes.

Add the pasta and simmer with the lid on for another 10 minutes.

Season with salt and pepper, finish with the chives and serve with Parmesan cheese.

AGA

Fry the vegetables on the simmering plate.
Bring the soup to the boil, cover with the lid and place in the slow cooking oven for 20 minutes.
Add the pasta and simmer with the lid on for another 10 minutes in the slow cooking oven.

TO SERVE 4

FOR THE FISH FUMET:
fish bones from 3 fish, rinsed well
4 tablespoons olive oil
3 carrots, cleaned and roughly chopped
1 fennel, cleaned and roughly chopped
3 celery stalks, cleaned and roughly chopped
1 leek, cleaned and roughly chopped
1 large onion, peeled and roughly chopped
2 cloves garlic, peeled and pressed
4 sprigs thyme
2 bay leaves
4 parsley stalks
140 g tomato paste
pepper and salt
1 dl pastis
2.5 dl white wine
1.5 litres water

FOR THE SOUP:
800 g mussels, cleaned
330 g clams, rinsed and cleaned
1 fillet of plaice, in pieces
1 fillet of sole, cut in pieces
1 fillet of gilt-head bream, cut in pieces
a few leaves of (red) basil

Fish soup with pastis

FISH FUMET
Sauté the fish bones in the olive oil in a large saucepan and add the coarsely chopped vegetables.

Add the garlic, thyme, bay leaf, parsley stems and tomato purée. Season with pepper and salt.

Deglaze with the pastis, white wine and water.

Leave to cook well for 25 minutes.

Strain the fumet through a straining cloth.

SOUP
Place the fumet on a low heat and add the shellfish and fish. Poach until everything is cooked.

Garnish the soup with the basil leaves.

AGA

Cook the vegetables and allow the fish fumet to cook thoroughly on the boiling plate.
Poach the fish, with the lid on, on the simmering plate or in the slow cooking oven.

PASTA & RICE

Casseroles with pasta and rice: always a hit

Delicious and a feast for the eyes: a beautiful casserole full of good things that you simply place in the middle of the table and let everyone serve themselves.
A fragrant pasta dish, perfectly cooked 'al dente' and filled with delicious things or topped with a colourful sauce ... a delight for young and old alike! Dishes with perfectly cooked rice in combination with meat or fish are also always a hit.
Conviviality surpasses!

TO SERVE 4

FOR THE FILLING:
2 shallots, peeled and shredded
3 cloves garlic, peeled and pressed
olive oil
1 pointed pepper, cleaned, seeded and diced
½ courgette, cleaned and diced
1 tablespoon Provençal herbs
1 teaspoon chilli flakes
1 teaspoon fennel seeds
500 g mixed minced meat
1 egg
pepper and salt

FOR THE TOMATO SAUCE:
1 large onion, peeled and shredded
1 clove garlic, peeled and pressed
dash of olive oil
50 g white wine
800 g tinned chopped tomatoes
1 teaspoon sugar
pinch of salt
5 basil leaves
1 bay leaf
1 sprig thyme

AND ALSO:
olive oil
16 cannelloni tubes
250 g ricotta
150 g Reypenaer cheese, grated
1 shallot, peeled and shredded
1 clove garlic, peeled and pressed
25 g butter
250 g spinach, washed
pepper and salt
nutmeg

Cannelloni

FILLING
Fry the shallot and garlic lightly in a drizzle of olive oil.

Add the pointed pepper and the courgette and leave to stew for a few minutes.

Place the stewed vegetables in a mixing bowl and allow to cool.

Mix the Provençal herbs, chilli flakes and fennel seeds with the vegetables.

Add the minced meat and the egg and season with salt and pepper. Mix everything well with your hands and placed the mixture into a piping bag.

SAUCE
Sauté the onion and garlic in a drizzle of olive oil.

Deglaze with the white wine and add the remaining ingredients.

Leave the sauce to simmer at a low heat.

CANNELLONI
Pre-heat the oven to 200 °C.

Grease an oven dish with olive oil.

Fill the cannelloni with the minced meat.

Arrange the cannelloni side by side in the oven dish.

Cover with the tomato sauce.

Spread the ricotta and the Reypenaer cheese over it.

Bake for 30 minutes in the pre-heated oven.

Fry the shallot and the garlic in the butter oil and add the spinach. Leave to cook briefly and season with nutmeg and pepper.

Serve the cannelloni with the spinach.

AGA

Cook the vegetables for the filling on the simmering plate.
Make the sauce on the simmering plate, cover with a lid and place in the slow cooking oven to simmer for 20 minutes.
Place the oven dish on the bottom of the roasting oven.
Cook the spinach on the simmering plate.

TO SERVE 4
1 fennel, cleaned, green parts separately
1 courgette, cleaned
1 clove garlic, peeled and pressed
4 tablespoons olive oil

pepper and salt
700 g salmon fillet
4 sprigs tarragon
70 g butter
80 g flour
5 dl fish stock

juice of 1 lemon

350 g green lasagne sheets
150 g mozzarella, finely grated
150 g Gruyère cheese, finely grated

Lasagne with salmon and fennel

Pre-heat the oven to 180 °C.

Cut the fennel and courgette into fine slices with the mandolin slicer.

Fry the fennel and courgette together with the garlic in the olive oil until golden brown. Season with pepper and salt. Reserve.

Slice the salmon fillets lengthwise with a fillet knife. Drizzle with olive oil, season with salt and pepper and top with the sprigs of tarragon. Reserve.

Melt the butter in a large saucepan and mix in the flour well. Leave the roux to dry. Add the fish stock, stirring all the time. Bring strongly to the boil and stir vigorously until you get a smooth sauce. Remove from the heat and add the lemon juice. Season with pepper and salt.

Spoon a third of the sauce into the bottom of the oven dish. Arrange a layer of lasagne sheets on top. Cover with half the salmon, the courgette and the fennel. Sprinkle with half the mozzarella and season with salt and pepper. Spoon another third of the sauce over the mozzarella and continue with lasagne sheets, salmon, courgette, fennel, mozzarella, salt and pepper and the rest of the sauce.

Sprinkle with the Gruyère cheese.

Bake for 35 minutes in the pre-heated oven.

Garnish with some extra tarragon and the green of the fennel.

AGA

Cook the vegetables on the simmering plate.
Make the sauce on the boiling plate.
Place the oven dish on the bottom of the baking oven.

TO SERVE 4

700 g parsnips, peeled and diced
4 + 4 tablespoons olive oil
3 sprigs thyme
pepper and salt

1 shallot, peeled and shredded
0.8 dl white wine
3 dl cream 40%
80 g pecorino, grated

80 g Bleu d'Auvergne, cut in pieces
80 g mozzarella, finely grated
80 g cheddar, finely grated
350 g lasagne sheets

Lasagne quattro formaggi

Pre-heat the oven to 180 °C.

Fry the parsnips in 4 tablespoons olive oil until brown. Add the thyme and season with salt and pepper. Reserve.

Stew the shallot in the same pan in 4 tablespoons olive oil.

Deglaze with the white wine and add the cream. Allow it to reduce well and remove the pan from the heat. Melt all the cheeses into the sauce and mix well. Season with pepper and salt.

Spoon a quarter of the sauce into the bottom of the oven dish. Follow with a layer of lasagne sheets and another layer of sauce. Divide half of the parsnip cubes over this. Cover with a layer of lasagne sheets, a layer of sauce, the rest of the parsnip cubes and the rest of the sauce.

Bake for 35 minutes in the pre-heated oven.

AGA

Use the simmering plate.
Place the oven dish in the centre of the baking oven.

TO SERVE 4

- 1 butternut squash, peeled (700 g pulp)
- 1 onion, peeled and shredded
- 1 clove garlic, peeled and pressed
- 4 tablespoons olive oil
- 250 g mushrooms, cleaned and sliced
- 80 g chorizo, skinned and diced
- 400 g spiced pork sausage meat, without skin
- 800 g tinned chopped tomatoes
- pepper and salt
- 500 g ricotta
- 0.8 dl milk
- leaves of 1 sprig of thyme
- 120 g pecorino, grated

Pumpkin lasagne

Pre-heat the oven to 180 °C.

Slice the butternut squash lengthwise into rings with the mandolin or mechanical slicer.

Sauté the onion and garlic in the olive oil.

Add the mushrooms, chorizo and sausage meat and leave to cook for a while.

Add the chopped tomatoes and season with salt and pepper.

Beat the ricotta with the milk and add the thyme and the pecorino. Season with pepper and salt.

Spoon half of the sauce into the bottom of the oven dish. Cover with slices of butternut squash and spread with half of the ricotta mixture. Repeat one more time and finish with the rest of the ricotta mixture.

Bake for 40 minutes in the pre-heated oven.

Check if the squash is cooked and, if necessary, cook a little longer.

AGA

Use the simmering plate.
Place the oven dish in the centre of the baking oven.

TO SERVE 4

8 merguez sausages
dash olive oil
1 onion, peeled and shredded
1 clove garlic, peeled and pressed
1 dl white wine
1 chilli pepper
1 bay leaf
2 sprigs thyme
16 sun-dried tomatoes in oil, drained
pepper and salt
400 g pasta foglie d'ulivo (in the shape of olive leaves, but you can use any type of pasta)
100 g Parmesan cheese, finely grated
250 g ricotta

Pasta with merguez

Fry the merguez in the olive oil until brown all over. Remove the sausages from the pan and reserve.

Sauté the onion and garlic in the fat from the merguez.

Deglaze with white wine and add the chilli pepper, bay leaf, thyme and sun-dried tomatoes. Season with pepper and salt. Leave to cook for 10 minutes.

Put the oven on grill setting.

Cook the pasta as instructed on the packaging.

Add the pasta to the sauce and mix.

Mix the Parmesan cheese with the ricotta. Season with pepper and salt.

Divide the pasta between individual oven dishes, arrange the merguez on top and sprinkle with the cheeses.

Leave to crust under the grill.

AGA

Fry the merguez on the boiling plate.
Stew the vegetables on the simmering plate.
Place the oven dish as high as possible in the roasting oven.

TO SERVE 4

FOR THE ARTICHOKE:
2 cans artichoke hearts, drained
1.5 dl olive oil
juice of 1 lemon
leaves of 2 sprigs of thyme
leaves of ½ bunch of flat parsley
3 cloves garlic, peeled and pressed

FOR THE PASTA SHELLS:
20 pasta shells
200 g kale, finely chopped, blanched and drained
2 cloves garlic, peeled and pressed
2 tablespoons olive oil
500 g ricotta
150 + 50 g Parmesan cheese, finely grated
leaves of 2 sprigs of thyme
pepper and salt
butter
70 g pine nuts, roasted

Pasta shells with kale and artichoke

ARTICHOKE
Marinate the artichoke in the olive oil and lemon juice with the thyme, parsley and garlic.

PASTA SHELLS
Pre-heat the oven to 220 °C.
Cook the pasta as instructed on the packaging and drain.

Fry the kale and garlic in the olive oil. Remove from heat and mix in the ricotta, 150 g Parmesan and thyme. Season with pepper and salt.

Arrange the cooked pasta shells in a buttered oven dish.

Fill the shells with the filling. Arrange the marinated artichoke on top and sprinkle with 50 g Parmesan cheese and the pine nuts.

Place the dish in the oven for a few minutes for the cheese to melt.

AGA

Cook the pasta on the boiling plate.
Stew the vegetables on the simmering plate.
Place the oven dish as high as possible in the roasting oven.

TO SERVE 4

- 8 dl chicken stock
- 1 shallot, peeled and shredded
- 1 clove garlic, peeled and shredded
- 0.25 dl olive oil
- 300 g Carnaroli rice
- ½ bottle champagne
- 70 g Parmesan cheese, grated
- 250 g ricotta
- 200 g crayfish tails, pre-cooked
- 50 g roquette
- pepper and salt

Champagne risotto with crayfish and ricotta

Pre-heat the oven to 180 °C.

Bring the chicken stock to the boil.

Sauté the shallot and garlic in the olive oil.

Add the rice and fry for 1 minute until all rice grains are covered with oil.

Deglaze with the champagne and leave to cook for a while. Add the chicken stock and bring to the boil. Season with pepper and salt.

Place the lid on the pan and place for 25 minutes in the pre-heated oven.

Remove the pan from the oven and stir in the Parmesan cheese and ricotta. Season with pepper and salt.

Serve the risotto with roquette and crayfish tails.

AGA

Bring the chicken stock to the boil on the boiling plate. Sauté the shallot, garlic and rice on the simmering plate. Place the risotto in the centre of the slow cooking oven.

TO SERVE 4

- 500 g cauliflower, in small florets
- butter for greasing baking pan
- 8 cherry tomatoes, halved
- 1 large onion, peeled and shredded
- 2 cloves garlic, peeled and shredded
- 2 tablespoons olive oil
- 200 g smoked bacon cubes
- 2 tablespoons olive oil
- 6 eggs
- 1 dl cream 40%
- 2 teaspoons mustard
- 1 tablespoon dried tarragon
- 1 tablespoon dried basil
- 1 tablespoon dried oregano
- 2 teaspoons soft paprika
- 1 pinch of cayenne pepper
- pepper and salt
- 100 g Emmental cheese, grated
- 20 leaves (purple) basil

Frittata with cauliflower

Pre-heat the oven to 180 °C.

Blanch the cauliflower florets for 5 minutes in boiling salted water. Cool under cold running water and drain.

Divide the cauliflower florets and cherry tomatoes across a 20 x 26 cm buttered baking tin.

Fry the onion and garlic gently in the olive oil. Add the bacon cubes and cook for 5 minutes. Divide over the baking pan.

Beat the eggs with the cream, mustard, dried herbs, paprika and cayenne pepper. Season with salt and pepper and beat the eggs until fluffy.

Pour the beaten eggs over the vegetables and sprinkle the Emmental cheese on top.

Bake for 30 minutes in the pre-heated oven.

Garnish with purple basil leaves.

AGA

Blanch the cauliflower on the boiling plate.
Fry the onion, garlic and bacon on the simmering plate.
Fry the frittata in the top of the baking oven.

POTATOES

Potatoes, a piece of food culture

When we opt for potatoes, we do it properly right from the start, using the tastiest varieties. We give a modern look to classics like pommes duchesse, gratin or buttermilk stampers. In the recipes we combine our potatoes with fresh herbs like bay leaves or serve them roasted. Creative variations on a product that we serve almost daily, and a pleasure to all that eat them!

FOR A Ø 28 CM PIE DISH

4 waxy potatoes, peeled and washed
5 dl whole milk
1 clove garlic, peeled and shredded
pepper and salt
nutmeg
1 sheet ready-made puff pastry
needles from 2 sprigs of rosemary
50 g Parmesan cheese, grated
100 g soured cream
½ red onion, peeled and sliced wafer-thin
1 egg yolk, beaten

Potato pie

Pre-heat the oven to 200 °C.

Cut the potatoes into fine slices with a mandolin slicer.

Bring the milk to the boil with the garlic and season with salt, pepper and nutmeg. Add the potato slices, cook for 10 minutes and drain.

Cover the pie dish with the puff pastry and pierce it with a fork.

Mix the rosemary, Parmesan cheese, soured cream and red onion and add the potatoes. Mix carefully.

Fill the pie dish with this mixture.

Brush the edges of the puff pastry with the beaten egg yolk.

Bake for 25 minutes in the pre-heated oven.

AGA

Cook the potatoes on the boiling plate.
Place the pie dish on the bottom of the roasting oven.

TO SERVE 4
FOR THE FRIES:
2.5 kg chip potatoes, peeled and cut into chips
1 dl peanut oil

FOR THE MAYONNAISE
1 egg
1 tablespoon mustard
3 dl grape seed oil
pepper and salt
pinch of cayenne pepper

1 teaspoon curry madras
10 drops Tabasco
juice of 1 lime

Oven fries with chilli mayonaise

Pre-heat the oven to 200 °C.

Blanch the chips for 5 minutes in boiling salted water

Drain and toss the chips in the peanut oil.

Place a sheet of baking paper or a baking mat on a baking tray and arrange the chips on top.

Bake for 15 minutes in the pre-heated oven.

Place all the mayonnaise ingredients except lime juice in a narrow mixing beaker. Place the hand blender on the bottom of the mixing bowl and mix until you get an emulsion. Now slowly pull the mixer upwards until you get the desired consistency. Add the lime juice and mix a little more.

AGA

Use the boiling plate;
Place the oven tray in the centre of the roasting oven.

TO SERVE 4
30 g fungi, dried
500 g waxy potatoes, peeled and washed
1.25 dl cream 40%
1 cup mushroom stock
4 tablespoons olive oil
pepper and salt
50 g bacon, sliced
10 sage leaves
1 clove garlic, peeled and pressed
100 g Parmesan cheese, finely grated

Potatoes with fungi, sage and bacon

Pre-heat the oven to 180 °C.

Soak the fungi in hot water for 10 minutes.

Cut the potatoes into 5 mm slices with a mandolin slicer.

Heat the cream and dissolve the mushroom stock into it.

Rub an oven dish with the olive oil and arrange potato slices in it so that they overlap.

Pour the cream over the potato slices and season with salt and pepper.

Divide the bacon, sage, garlic and soaked mushrooms over it.

Sprinkle with the Parmesan cheese.

Bake for 45 minutes in the pre-heated oven.

AGA

Heat the cream on the simmering plate.
Place the oven dish on the bottom of the baking oven.

TO SERVE 4
4 dl whole milk
4 dl cream 40%
2 cloves garlic, peeled
2 bay leaves
2 sprigs thyme
pepper and salt

nutmeg
800 g waxy potatoes, peeled
50 g butter, melted
200 g Gruyère cheese, finely grated

Potato gratin

Pre-heat the oven to 160 °C.

Bring the milk to the boil with the cream, garlic, bay leaves and thyme and season with salt, pepper and nutmeg. Remove from the heat and leave to draw for at least minimum 15 minutes.

Cut the potatoes into fine slices with a mandolin slicer.

Grease the oven dish with melted butter and arrange a layer of overlapping potato slices over it. Brush with melted butter again and do the same for the second and third layers or until all the potato slices are used up.

Strain the milk over the potatoes.

If necessary, season further with pepper and salt.

Sprinkle with the Gruyère cheese.

Bake for 30 minutes in the pre-heated oven.

AGA

Bring the milk to the boil on the boiling plate.
Place the oven dish on the bottom of the baking oven.

TO SERVE 4

1 large onion, peeled and sliced
2 cloves garlic, peeled and pressed
4 tablespoons olive oil
750 g waxy potatoes, peeled
1 kg Roma tomatoes
butter for greasing the oven dish
pepper and salt
3 dl vegetable stock
leaves of 2 sprigs of thyme
20 basil leaves
1 tablespoon roasted sesame seeds
1 tablespoon honey

Potatoes with tomato crust

Pre-heat the oven to 200 °C.

Sauté the onion and garlic in the olive oil.

Cut the potatoes into 5 millimetre slices with a mandolin slicer.

Cut the tomatoes into 5 millimetre slices.

Arrange the potato slices in a buttered oven dish overlappingly. Spread the sautéed onion on top and then the tomato slices. Season with pepper and salt.

Bring the vegetable stock to the boil and pour over the tomatoes.

Spread the thyme and basil leaves over the tomatoes.

Cover the oven dish with aluminium foil

Bake for 45 minutes in the pre-heated oven.

Remove the aluminium foil and return to the oven for 15 minutes until the potatoes are tender and the tomatoes have a burnt edge.

Check that the potatoes are cooked and if necessary place back in the oven for a little longer.

Sprinkle with the toasted sesame seeds and finish with a hint of honey.

AGA

Use the boiling plate.
Place the oven dish for 45 minutes in the centre of the roasting oven.
Place the oven dish for 15 minutes as high as possible in the roasting oven.

TO SERVE 4
1 kg waxy potatoes, peeled and washed
pepper and salt
4 spring onions, cleaned and cut into thin rings
60 g smoked bacon, cubed
40 g butter, cut into chunks
250 g mozzarella, drained and chopped
1 clove garlic, peeled, pressed and mixed with 1 tablespoon olive oil
20 basil leaves

Potato dish with mozzarella

Pre-heat the oven to 180 °C.

Boil the potatoes in plenty of salted water for 20 minutes until cooked and drain.

Place a sheet of baking paper in a baking tray and arrange the potatoes on top.

Push down on the top of the potatoes with the back of a spoon so that they pop open slightly. Season with pepper and salt.

Divide the spring onion, bacon, butter, mozzarella and garlic oil over the potatoes.

Bake in the pre-heated oven for 10 minutes until the cheese has melted and the potatoes are golden brown.

Garnish with basil leaves.

AGA

Bring the potatoes to the boil on the boiling plate, drain and cook, with the lid on, in the centre of the slow cooking oven for 20 minutes.
Place the oven dish in the roasting oven.

TO SERVE 4
8 waxy potatoes, peeled
8 tablespoons olive oil
100 g butter, cut in pieces
pepper and salt

7 dl chicken stock
6 cloves garlic, peeled
4 sprigs thyme

Fondant potatoes

Pre-heat the oven to 220 °C.

Cut the potatoes into 3-centimetre slices. Cut out circles with a ring or cut them by hand into 'barrels'. Rinse under cold water.

Heat the olive oil and butter in a cast iron pan and place the potato rounds upright in the pan. Season with pepper and salt.

Brown the bottom and turn the potato rounds over.

Add the chicken stock until the potato rounds are two thirds under. Bring to the boil.

Add the garlic and little thyme.

Bake for 30 minutes in the pre-heated oven.

AGA

Cook the potatoes on the boiling plate.
Place the pan as high as possible in the roasting oven.

TO SERVE 4
800 g floury potatoes, peeled and cut into chunks
dash of milk
40 g butter
1 egg yolk
pepper and salt
nutmeg
butter for greasing the ramekins
2 tablespoons breadcrumbs
16 small lumps of butter
4 bratwursts, baked

Gratinated potato puree with sausages

Pre-heat the oven to 200 °C.

Cook the potatoes in well-salted water. Drain and leave on the hot stove to dry.

Puree the potatoes and add the milk, butter and egg yolk. Mix well and season with pepper, salt and nutmeg.

Divide the purée between four individual buttered oven dishes and smooth.

Sprinkle with the breadcrumbs and distribute four small lumps of butter over each dish.

Press a fried sausage into each dish of puree.

Bake in the pre-heated oven for a few minutes until the purée has a golden-brown, crispy crust.

AGA

Bring the potatoes to the boil on the boiling plate, drain and cook, with the lid on, in the centre of the slow cooking oven for 20 minutes.
Place the oven dishes as high as possible in the roasting oven.

TO SERVE 4

2 tablespoons Himalaya salt
1 tablespoon dried tarragon
1 tablespoon Provençal herbs
4 large floury potatoes,
peeled and washed
2 tablespoons olive oil

Roast potatoes

Pre-heat the oven to 180 °C.

Mix the salt with the tarragon and the Provençal herbs.

Place half the mixture on the bottom of an oven dish.

Brush the potatoes with the oil and arrange them on the seasoning salt.

Cover with the rest of the seasoning salt.

Roast the potatoes in the pre-heated oven for 75 minutes until blistered and very soft and crumbly on the inside.

AGA

Roast the potatoes in the centre of the baking oven.

TO SERVE 4
4 sweet potatoes, washed
2 tablespoons olive oil
pepper and coarse sea salt
4 chicken legs
8 slices pancetta
125 g fresh goat's cheese
4 sprigs curly parsley
1 chilli, without seeds and in fine rings

Roast sweet potatoes with chicken

Pre-heat the oven to 200 °C.

Place each potato on a sheet of aluminium foil. Prick holes in the potato with a potato skewer. Drizzle with the olive oil and season with pepper and coarse sea salt. Wrap the aluminium foil right round and arrange the potatoes in an oven dish.

Season the chicken legs with salt and pepper and fry in a cast iron pan until golden brown all over.

Place the oven dish with the potatoes and the cast iron pan with the chicken legs in the pre-heated oven for 30 minutes.

Fry the pancetta until crispy in a pan without extra fat. Reserve.

Remove the potato from the oven, loosen the aluminium foil and make an indentation with a knife in the top of the potato.

Finish with a slice of fresh goat's cheese, 2 slices of pancetta, a sprig of parsley and chilli pepper.

Serve with a chicken leg.

AGA

Roast the sweet potatoes in the centre of the baking oven.
Bake the chicken legs on a second rack in the oven.
Fry the pancetta on the boiling plate.

TO SERVE 4

12 Ratte potatoes
butter for greasing the oven dish
leaves of 8 sprigs of flat parsley
12 sprigs thyme
1 tablespoon flake salt
4 tablespoons olive oil
60 bay leaves
4 sprigs rosemary
1 full bulb fresh garlic, peeled and quartered
8 carrots, cleaned
8 black peppercorns
soured cream

Hasselback potatoes with bay leaves

Pre-heat the oven to 200 °C.

Wash the potatoes thoroughly.

Take 2 cutting boards of the same height or 2 wooden spoons and clamp a potato between them. Slice each potato 5 times. The cutting boards or the wooden spoons ensure that you do not cut the potato completely.

Arrange the potatoes cut side up in a buttered oven dish.

Put the parsley leaves together with the fermented leaves of 6 sprigs of thyme in a mortar. Add the salt and grind with the pestle to a smooth paste.

Add the olive oil and mix well.

Brush the potatoes generously with the mixture, also between the cuts.

Stick 5 bay leaves per potato into the cuts.

Sprinkle the remaining sprigs of thyme and rosemary, garlic, carrots and peppercorns over the potatoes.

Bake in the pre-heated oven for 40 minutes until crispy on the outside and well-cooked on the inside. Larger potatoes need a little longer, smaller potatoes a little less.

Remove the bay leaves and serve the hasselback potatoes with a spoonful of soured cream.

AGA

Place the oven dish on the bottom of the roasting oven.

TO SERVE 4

600 g floury potatoes, peeled	salt
200 g parsnips, peeled and cubed	nutmeg
150 g butter	40 g flaked almonds
3 + 1 egg yolks	

Duchesse potatoes with parsnips

Put the oven on grill setting.

Cook the potatoes for 10 minutes in well-salted water.

Add the parsnips and leave to boil for another 10 minutes.

Drain and grind through the passe-vite, to end up with a fine purée.

Stir the butter with 3 egg yolks into the purée and season with salt and nutmeg.

Spoon the puree into a piping bag with a wide serrated nozzle.

Place a sheet of baking paper or a baking mat on a baking tray.

Pipe the puree into identical swirls approximately 4 centimetres wide and high.

Beat the remaining egg yolk and brush the swirls with it.

Sprinkle with flaked almonds.

Place under the grill for 10-15 minutes until the edges are golden brown.

AGA

Place the baking tray as high as possible in the roasting oven.

TO SERVE 4
1 thick slice white bread, without crust, cut into small chunks
25 g + 60 g butter
500 g floury potatoes, peeled and cut into chunks
2 dl buttermilk
pepper and salt
nutmeg
4 eggs
150 g peeled shrimps

Buttermilk stampers

Fry the chunks of white bread in 25 grams of butter until golden brown. Reserve.

Cook the potatoes in well-salted water.

Drain and grind through the passe-vite, to end up with a fine purée.

Melt 60 grams of butter in a pan until it turns hazelnut brown.

Add the hazelnut-brown butter and buttermilk and season with pepper, salt and nutmeg.

Boil the eggs softly for 5 minutes.

Carefully peel the eggs and arrange them on the buttermilk purée.

Garnish with the shrimps and bread chunks.

AGA

Use the boiling plate;
Bring the potatoes to the boil on the boiling plate, drain and cook, with the lid on, in the centre of the slow cooking oven for 20 minutes.

TO SERVE 4

FOR THE PUREE:
4 leeks, cleaned and in rings
30 + 50 g butter
600 g floury potatoes, peeled and diced
3 egg yolks
pepper and salt

FOR THE SAUCE:
1 dl white martini
1 dl fish stock
1 shallot, peeled and halved
1 bay leaf
2 sprigs thyme
1 tablespoon pink pepper, dried
4 white peppercorns
pinch of salt
3 dl cream 40%
juice of ½ lemon
1 bunch chives, finely chopped

FOR THE GARNISH:
200 g freshly-peeled shrimp

Parmentier with shrimps

Pre-heat the oven to 120 °C.

Fry the leeks in 30 grams of butter. Reserve.

Cook the potatoes in well-salted water.

Drain and grind through the passe-vite, to end up with a fine purée.

Stir the 50 grams of butter with the egg yolks into the purée.

Mix the fried leek and the cooking liquid into the purée. Season with pepper and salt.

Divide the purée into individual oven dishes.

Bake for 15 minutes in the pre-heated oven.

Bring the martini, the fish stock, the shallot, the bay leaf, the thyme, the pink pepper and the peppercorns to the boil in a pan, season with salt and reduce by half.

Pass through a sieve, add the cream and reduce again to a creamy sauce.

Finish with the lemon juice and chives.

Remove the purée from the oven, divide the shrimps between the oven dishes and serve with the sauce.

AGA

Cook the leek on the boiling plate.
Bring the potatoes to the boil on the boiling plate, drain and cook, with the lid on, in the centre of the slow cooking oven for 20 minutes.
Place the individual oven dishes in the centre of the simmering oven.

VEGGIE

Veggie, surprisingly delicious

The oven is the appliance par excellence for preparing the tastiest veggie dishes. In the evenly distributed heat, the dishes cook gently both above and below and the flavours remain pure. A slightly less well-known method, but definitely worth the trouble: cooking larger vegetables such as cauliflower or pumpkin whole and working them into your dishes afterwards.

TO SERVE 4

1 butternut squash, halved lengthwise and seeded
olive oil
pepper and salt
2 cloves garlic, peeled and sliced + 1 clove garlic, peeled
75 g dried brown lentils, soaked
1 bay leaf
1 onion, peeled and shredded
needles from 1 sprig of rosemary, finely chopped
300 g kale leaves, trimmed and cut into 1 cm wide strands
150 g herb cheese
8 slices processed cheddar cheese

Butternut with kale stuffing

Pre-heat the oven to 200 °C.

Place the squash cut side up in an oven dish and score the flesh with a knife. Rub 2 tablespoons olive oil into each side and season with salt and pepper.

Press the slices of garlic into the pulp of the squash.

Cover the oven dish with aluminium foil and bake for 40 minutes in the pre-heated oven.

Boil the soaked lentils for 20 minutes in plenty of water with the bay leaf and the remaining garlic clove until tender. Pour off the cooking water and leave to drain.

Sauté the onion, kale and rosemary in two tablespoons olive oil for 10 minutes. Season with pepper and salt.

Remove the squash from the oven.

Increase the oven temperature to 220 °C.

Carefully spoon the pulp out of the squash without damaging the skin. Place the pulp in a mixing bowl and allow to cool a little.

Mix the kale, lentils and herb cheese into the squash. Season with pepper and salt.

Fill the squash skins with the mixture and top with the cheddar.

Place the dish in the pre-heated oven for 4 minutes for the cheese to melt.

AGA

Place the oven dish with the squash in the top of the baking oven.
Place the cheese to melt in the middle of the roasting oven.

TIP

The aluminium foil creates a steaming effect, which shortens the cooking time.
Replace the cooked lentils with 600 g baked ground beef for a non-vegetarian variety.

TO SERVE 4

800 g beans of your choice, dried and soaked overnight in cold water

600 g cherry tomatoes

olive oil

1 red onion, peeled and shredded

4 cloves garlic, peeled and shredded

0.5 dl white wine

2 sprigs thyme

1 teaspoon sambal

2 tablespoons tomato ketchup

pepper and salt

Bean dish

Pre-heat the oven to 120 °C.

Bring the beans, with the water in which they have soaked, to the boil and leave to boil for a few minutes until well cooked.

Cook the beans in the pre-heated oven with the lid on the pan according to the instructions on the package. Depending on the type of beans, this can take between 1 and 3 hours.

Pour off the cooking water and leave the beans to drain.

Place the tomatoes, onion and garlic in a mixing bowl. Pour over the white wine and drizzle generously with olive oil. Add the thyme, sambal and tomato ketchup and season with salt and pepper. Mix everything well.

Add the cooked beans and mix again.

Brush an oven dish with olive oil and fill with the bean mixture.

Bake for 25 minutes in the pre-heated oven.

AGA

Boil the beans on the simmering plate.
Cook the beans on the bottom of the slow cooking oven.
Place the oven dish on the bottom of the roasting oven.

TO SERVE 4
4 aubergines
butter for greasing oven dish
salt
570 g burrata, drained

4 tomatoes, peeled, seeded and diced
leaves of 2 sprigs thyme
pepper
30 fresh red baby leaves

Burrata with roasted aubergine

Cut the aubergines in half lengthwise and sprinkle with plenty of salt. Leave for 30 minutes, rinse and pat dry. Place in a buttered oven dish.

Pre-heat the oven to 180 °C.

Bake for 17 minutes in the pre-heated oven.

Remove the aubergines from the oven and spread the burrata, the diced tomato and the thyme over it. Season with pepper.

Place the oven dish back in the oven for 10 minutes. Serve with fresh red baby leaves

AGA

Place the oven dish on the bottom of the roasting oven.

TIP

We salt the aubergines to make cooking easier.

TO SERVE 4

FOR THE SAUCE
150 g Greek yoghurt
1 tablespoon tahini (sesame paste)
10 mint leaves, finely chopped
50 g cucumber, finely chopped and squeezed
dash of white wine
pepper and salt

FOR THE STRUDEL
250 g mushrooms of your choice, cleaned and sliced
2 tablespoons olive oil
125 g baby spinach, washed
pepper and salt
4 sheets filo pastry
extra olive oil for coating filo pastry

100 g Parmesan cheese, crumbled
1 red onion, peeled and cut into strips
¼ pointed pepper, shredded
handful of oak leaf lettuce

Mushroom strudel with spinach

SAUCE
Mix all ingredients and store them covered in the refrigerator.

STRUDEL
Pre-heat the oven to 180 °C.

Fry the mushrooms in the olive oil until tender.

Add the spinach and leave to stew for about three minutes. Season with pepper and salt.

Pour off the cooking water and drain through a sieve.

Place a sheet of baking paper or a baking mat on a baking tray.

Place a sheet of filo pastry on the baking tray. Brush with olive oil and place a second sheet on top. Brush again with olive oil and place the third sheet on top. Brush one last time with olive oil and place the fourth sheet on top.

Spoon the mixture into the centre of the pastry and fold the pastry together with the top and bottom facing each other. Fold the sides neatly under the roll.

Brush the top of the strudel with olive oil.

Bake for 30 minutes in the pre-heated oven.

Remove the strudel from the oven and cut a rectangle out of the top.

Finish with the Parmesan cheese, the red onion, the pointed pepper and the oak leaf lettuce.

Serve with the sauce.

AGA

Fry the mushrooms and stew the spinach on the simmering plate.
Place the baking tray in the middle of the baking oven.

TO SERVE 4
1 red onion, peeled and sliced
2 cloves garlic, peeled and shredded
25 g butter
1 pointed pepper, trimmed, seeded and in rings
100 g spinach, washed
400 g tinned chopped tomatoes
400 g tinned chickpeas, drained
2 teaspoons ras el hanout
4.5 dl poultry stock
15 g sugar
pepper and salt
400 g mashed potatoes
1 tablespoon breadcrumbs
150 g Emmental cheese, grated

Cottage pie

Pre-heat the oven to 200 °C.

Stew the kale and garlic in the butter. Add the paprika and spinach and cook together for a while.

Add the chopped tomatoes, chickpeas, ras el hanout, poultry stock and sugar and season with salt and pepper.

Distribute the mixture between four individual buttered oven dishes.

Place a layer of mashed potatoes on top and smooth.

Sprinkle with the breadcrumbs and Emmentaler.

Bake for 15 minutes in the pre-heated oven.

AGA

Stew the vegetables on the simmering plate. Place the individual oven dishes on the bottom of the roasting oven.

FOR ONE CAULIFLOWER

1 cauliflower, cleaned
50 g butter, melted
1 teaspoon curry powder
pinch of cayenne pepper
2 teaspoons garlic paste
pepper and salt
nutmeg

Roasted cauliflower

Pre-heat the oven to 200 °C.

Place a sheet of baking paper or a baking mat on a baking tray.

Cut the bottom of the cauliflower flat and place on a baking tray.

Mix the melted butter with the curry powder, the cayenne pepper and the garlic paste. Season with pepper and salt.

Brush the cauliflower with the spice butter.

Roast for 40 minutes in the pre-heated oven.

Remove the cauliflower from the oven and sprinkle some more nutmeg over it.

AGA

Roast the cauliflower on the bottom of the roasting oven.

TO SERVE 4

2 round pumpkins of approx. 1800 g each

10 sage leaves

50 g butter

pepper and salt

Roasted pumpkin

Pre-heat the oven to 200 °C.

Roast the pumpkins for 75 minutes in the pre-heated oven.

Check that they are tender and leave to cool.

Cut off the top of the pumpkins, cut in half and remove the seeds.

Spoon the pulp from the pumpkins and purée in a blender.

Roll up a number of sage leaves and cut into fine strings. Fry them briefly in the butter and add the pumpkin purée. Season with pepper and salt.

Serve with small pieces of bread.

AGA

Place the pumpkins on a grid on the bottom of the roasting oven.

TO SERVE 4

400 g kohlrabi, washed
butter for greasing the oven dish
100 g spinach
pepper and salt and nutmeg
200 g Roquefort
1 clove garlic, peeled and pressed
2.5 dl cream 40%

Kohlrabi gratin

Pre-heat the oven to 180 °C.

Cut the kohlrabi with the mandolin slicer into 3 millimetre slices.

Place a layer of overlapping kohlrabi slices in a buttered oven dish.

Cover with the spinach, season with salt, pepper and nutmeg and place another layer of overlapping kohlrabi slices on top of the spinach.

Crumble the Roquefort cheese over the kohlrabi.

Spread the garlic across the oven dish and pour the cream on top. Season with pepper and salt.

Cook for 20 minutes in the pre-heated oven until tender.

Check whether the kohlrabi is tender, and if necessary return to the oven for a bit longer.

AGA

Place the oven dish on the bottom of the roasting oven.

TO SERVE 4

1 red onion, peeled and shredded
1 clove garlic, peeled and pressed
2 tablespoons olive oil
1 red pointed pepper, cleaned, seeded and diced
350 g quorn (vegetarian minced meat)
230 g taco sauce
150 g tinned sweet corn, drained
160 g tinned kidney beans, drained
1 teaspoon ras el hanout
1 teaspoon cumin seeds
pepper and salt
1 jalapeño peppers, drained and diced
200 g vegan cheese, grated
1 bag of tortilla chips
zest of 1 lime

Mexican vegetable dish

Pre-heat the oven to 180 °C.

Fry the red onion and garlic in the olive oil.

Add the pointed paprika and continue to fry.

Add the quorn and simmer.

Add the taco sauce, sweet corn, kidney beans, ras el hanout and cumin seeds. Season with pepper and salt and mix everything well.

Add the jalapeño peppers and half of the vegan cheese and mix.

Brush an oven dish with olive oil and add the mixture to the dish. Spread the chips across the dish.

Sprinkle with the rest of the vegan cheese.

Bake for 10 minutes in the pre-heated oven.

Sprinkle with the lime zest.

AGA

Stew the vegetables on the simmering plate.
Place the oven dish in the middle of the baking oven.

FOR 16 ROLLS

2 leek stems, cleaned and sliced
1 shallot, peeled and shredded
2 tablespoons olive oil
200 g Parmesan cheese, finely grated
85 g butter, at room temperature
500 g self-raising flour
1 teaspoon dried sage
2 eggs
pepper and salt
2 dl buttermilk

Leek rolls

Pre-heat the oven to 180 °C.

Sauté the leeks and shallot in the olive oil.

Place in a mixing bowl and add the Parmesan cheese. Mix well.

Place the butter, flour, sage and 1 egg in a second mixing bowl and season with salt and pepper. Knead into a crumbly dough.

Now add the buttermilk together with the fried leek and knead into a homogeneous dough.

Roll out the dough 2 centimetres thick on a floured work surface.

Cut the dough into 16 squares.

Place a sheet of baking paper or a baking mat on a baking tray and arrange the squares on top.

Beat the remaining egg well and brush the dough with it.

Bake for 30 minutes in the pre-heated oven until golden brown.

AGA

Stew the vegetables on the simmering plate. Place the baking tray in the middle of the baking oven.

TO SERVE 4

- 1 radicchio, outer leaves removed and leaves detached
- 400 g ricotta
- 40 g walnuts, chopped
- 2 egg yolks
- 40 + 100 g Parmesan cheese, grated
- pepper and salt
- butter for greasing oven dishes
- olive oil
- 4 fresh figs, halved lengthways
- 4 tablespoons honey
- 20 basil leaves

Radicchio with ricotta

Pre-heat the oven to 200 °C.

Blanch the radicchio leaves for a few minutes in boiling salted water Cool under cold running water and drain.

Mix the ricotta, nuts, egg yolks and 40 grams of Parmesan cheese in a mixing bowl. Season with pepper and salt.

Pat the radicchio leaves dry and fill them with the ricotta mixture. Roll up the leaves tightly with the filling and tie with kitchen twine. Make sure you have 8 rolls.

Arrange 2 rolls each in little buttered oven dishes and drizzle with olive oil.

Arrange the figs on the oven dishes. Drizzle with the honey.

Divide the basil leaves over the little oven dishes and sprinkle with 100 grams of Parmesan cheese.

Bake for 15 minutes in the pre-heated oven.

AGA

Blanch the radicchio on the boiling plate. Place the baking tray on the bottom of the roasting oven.

PIZZA

Pizza à gogo

A delicious dish that invariably creates a warm atmosphere around the table in our home: a homemade pizza with full, fresh ingredients. In composing my pizzas I have two basic rules I never deviate from: the recipe for my pizza dough that always succeeds and a freshly made passata. For the topping I only have one golden piece of advice: let your creativity run free and experiment to your heart's content with whatever you have in the house. Buon appetito!

Pizza with ceps and quail egg

FOR 1 PIZZA
1 fresh pizza base
1 dl fresh passata
pepper and salt
½ white sweet onion, peeled and shredded
1 cep, cleaned and sliced
12 chanterelle mushrooms, cleaned
3 quail eggs
150 g Comté cheese, grated

Pre-heat the oven to 240 °C.

Brush the pizza base with the passata, keeping 2 centimetres away from the edge. Season with pepper and salt.

Spread the onion and mushrooms over the pizza base.

Break the eggs in 3 places on the pizza.

Sprinkle with the Comté.

Bake for 15 minutes in the pre-heated oven.

AGA

Place the pizza on a pizza shovel and bake directly on the bottom of the roasting oven.

Basic dough for pizza

FOR 1 PIZZA
200 g 00 flour
2 tablespoons olive oil
1 teaspoon salt
18 g fresh yeast
100 g lukewarm water

Mix the flour, olive oil and salt in a food processor with a dough hook.

Dissolve the yeast in the water and add to the flour.

Knead into a smooth, homogeneous dough.

Place the dough on a floured wooden board and roll into a ball. Cover with a damp cloth and leave to rise for 90 minutes.

Roll out the dough into a nice round pizza base.

FOR 1 PIZZA
1 fresh pizza base
1 dl fresh passata
pepper and salt
½ white sweet onion, peeled and shredded
12 broccoli florets, blanched
a handful of young spinach leaves
1 tablespoon green pesto
150 g mozzarella, finely grated

Pizza with broccoli and spinach

Pre-heat the oven to 240 °C.

Brush the pizza base with the passata, keeping 2 centimetres away from the edge. Season with pepper and salt.

Divide the onion, broccoli, spinach and pesto over the pizza base.

Sprinkle with the mozzarella.

Bake for 15 minutes in the pre-heated oven.

AGA

Place the pizza on a pizza shovel and bake directly on the bottom of the roasting oven.

TIP

To blanch, cook the vegetables for a short time over a high heat without a lid, drain and rinse under cold running water to stop the cooking process.

FOR 1 PIZZA
1 fresh pizza base
1 dl fresh passata
pepper and salt
½ white sweet onion, peeled and shredded
6 slices pancetta, finely chopped
15 basil leaves
1 teaspoon dried oregano
100 g raclette cheese, cut into pieces without crust
50 g mozzarella cheese, finely grated
50 g Old Bruges cheese, in small blocks

Pizza raclette

Pre-heat the oven to 240 °C.

Brush the pizza base with the passata, keeping 2 centimetres away from the edge. Season with pepper and salt.

Spread the onion, pancetta and basil over the pizza base.

Sprinkle with the oregano and cheeses.

Bake for 15 minutes in the pre-heated oven.

AGA

Place the pizza on a pizza shovel and bake directly on the bottom of the roasting oven.

FOR 1 PIZZA
1 fresh pizza base
1 dl fresh passata
pepper and salt
½ red onion, peeled and shredded
4 sun-dried tomatoes
1 fine slices pancetta
2 teaspoons dried oregano
150 g mozzarella, finely grated

Pizza pancetta

Pre-heat the oven to 240 °C.

Brush the pizza base with the passata, keeping 2 centimetres away from the edge. Season with pepper and salt.

Spread the red onion, the sun-dried tomatoes and pancetta over the pizza base.

Sprinkle with the oregano and mozzarella.

Bake for 15 minutes in the pre-heated oven.

TRAYBAKE

Tray bake, pure and simple

Tray bake dishes are perhaps the aroma toppers par excellence. They are also super easy to make and the possibilities are endless. The name says everything: put all your ingredients onto a baking tray, sprinkle generously with fresh herbs and olive oil and slide into the oven … The result is delicious! The choice of ingredients is completely yours: have chicken, cheese, meat or fish play the leading role, or go for a pure vegetable mix.

TO SERVE 4

20 young carrots with leaves, cut and halved lengthwise
500 g new potatoes, washed and halved
3 tablespoons olive oil
2 teaspoons cumin seeds
pepper and flake salt
8 chipolata sausages
20 mini green asparagus, cleaned
8 stalks of broccolini, cleaned
100 g feta cheese, crumbled
zest of 1 orange

Tray bake with young carrots and chipolatas

Pre-heat the oven to 200 °C.

Mix the carrots and new potatoes with the olive oil and arrange them on an oven tray. Sprinkle with the cumin seeds and season with pepper and flake salt.

Add the chipolata sausages.

Bake for 20 minutes in the pre-heated oven.

Remove the oven tray from the oven and reduce the temperature to 180 ° C.

Spread the asparagus, broccolini, feta cheese and orange zest over the carrots and new potatoes.

Return the tray to the oven and cook for 10 minutes.

AGA

Place the oven tray the first time round on the bottom of the roasting oven.
Place the oven tray the second time round on the bottom of the baking oven.

TO SERVE 4

4 chicken legs
olive oil
1 teaspoon chicken seasoning
pepper
pinch of celery salt
300 g sweet peppers, without seeds and cut into strings
250 g cherry tomatoes, halved
2 red onions, peeled and cut into fine rings
2 cloves garlic, peeled and thinly sliced
200 g mushrooms, cleaned
zest of 1 lemon, lemon in wedges
100 g Kalamata olives
flake salt

Tray bake with chicken and paprika

Pre-heat the oven to 200 °C.

Rub the chicken legs with the olive oil, chicken spices, pepper and celery salt.

Arrange the legs on the oiled baking tray.

Bake for 25 minutes in the pre-heated oven.

Remove the tray from the oven and lower the temperature to 180 °C.

Spread the paprika, cherry tomatoes, red onion, garlic, mushrooms, lemon zest, lemon wedges and olives over the baking tray.

Drizzle generously with olive oil and season with flaked salt.

Bake for 20 minutes in the pre-heated oven.

AGA

Place the oven tray the first time round in the middle of the roasting oven.
Place the oven tray the second time round on the bottom of the baking oven.

TO SERVE 4

- 250 g carrots, cleaned and sliced
- 2 red onions, peeled, halved and pulled apart
- 1 tablespoon fennel seeds
- 4 tablespoons olive oil + extra
- 600 g skinless salmon fillet
- 1 tin white beans, rinsed and drained
- pepper and salt
- 1 lemon, in wedges
- 1 bok choy, cleaned and divided into leaves
- 100 g young spinach, washed
- 4 sprigs thyme
- flake salt
- 4 sprigs curly parsley, washed

Tray bake with salmon, carrot and bok choy

Pre-heat the oven to 200 °C.

Mix the carrots and onion with 4 tablespoons olive oil and the fennel seeds.

Arrange the carrots and onion on a baking tray.

Bake for a few minutes in the pre-heated oven.

Remove the tray from the oven and lower the temperature to 180 °C.

Season the salmon fillet with salt and pepper and place along with the white beans, lemon wedges, bok choy leaves, spinach and thyme sprigs with the carrots and onion on the baking tray.

Drizzle generously with olive oil and season with flaked salt.

Bake for 10 to 15 minutes in the pre-heated oven.

Finish with some curly parsley.

AGA

Place the oven tray the first time round on the bottom of the roasting oven.
Place the oven tray the second time round in the middle of the baking oven.

TO SERVE 4

400 g sweet potato, peeled and washed
½ fennel, sliced
2 red onions, peeled and quartered
½ fennel, cleaned
4 cloves garlic, unpeeled
needles from 1 sprig rosemary, finely chopped + 5 sprigs rosemary
olive oil
pepper
flake salt
1 teaspoon dried oregano
250 g wild mushrooms, cleaned and halved
250 g ricotta
zest 1 lime

Tray bake with sweet potato, fennel and ricotta

Pre-heat the oven to 200 °C.

Remove balls from the sweet potato with a Parisian scoop.

Mix with the fennel, onion, garlic, rosemary needles, 4 tablespoons olive oil and season with pepper and flaky salt.

Spread across an oven tray. Arrange the rosemary sprigs on top and sprinkle with the oregano. Add a little more olive oil if needed.

Bake for 15 minutes in the pre-heated oven.

Clean and halve the mushrooms.

Remove the tray from the oven and lower the temperature to 170 °C.

Spread the mushrooms and the ricotta across the baking tray and sprinkle with the lime zest. Drizzle with olive oil.

Bake for 10 minutes in the pre-heated oven.

AGA

Place the oven tray the first time round on the bottom of the roasting oven.
Place the oven tray the second time round on the bottom of the baking oven.

FISH

Fish, richness from the sea

A winner with many, super healthy and quick to prepare. Just sprinkle a bowl of fish and vegetables generously with olive oil and herbs, put it all in the oven... and leave the oven to do its job. Fresh fish and vegetables are of course an absolute must. Because the eye also wants something, you can opt for real pepper, full shallots and larger pieces of garlic.

TO SERVE 4

FOR THE PESTO
1 tablespoon hazelnuts, peeled
1 tablespoon cashews
10 basil leaves
3 tablespoons goat's cheese
pepper and salt
olive oil
juice of ½ lime

FOR THE FISH
2 courgettes, cleaned and diced
1 red pepper, seeded and diced
2 red onions, peeled and diced
4 tablespoons olive oil
3 cloves garlic, peeled and shredded
4 sprigs thyme
2 bay leaves
pepper and salt
4 daurade (gilt-head bream) fillets
250 g cherry tomatoes, halved
1 lemon, finely sliced
dash of olive oil

Dorade with ratatouille and pesto

PESTO
Mix all ingredients into a smooth pesto. Reserve.

FISH
Pre-heat the oven to 190 °C.

Fry the courgette, paprika pepper and onion in the olive oil and add the garlic, thyme and bay leaves. Season with pepper and salt.

Season the daurade fillets with pepper and salt.

Place the fried vegetables in an oven dish and arrange the daurade fillets on top. Add the cherry tomatoes and the lemon slices.

Bake for 7 minutes in the pre-heated oven.

Serve with the pesto.

AGA

Stew the vegetables on the simmering plate.
Place the oven dish on the bottom of the roasting oven.

TO SERVE 4

- 4 skinless cod fillets, 150 g each
- pepper and salt
- 2 shallots, peeled and quartered lengthways
- 2 cloves garlic, not peeled
- 1 chilli, seeded and cut lengthwise in eight
- 4 sprigs tarragon
- 4 sprigs thyme
- 20 basil leaves
- 10 cardamom seeds
- 1 star anise
- 8 black peppercorns
- 12 juniper berries
- flake salt
- 1 l grape seed oil

Glazed cod

Pre-heat the oven to 50 °C.

Season the cod with salt and pepper and arrange in a deep oven dish.

Spread the other ingredients on top of the fish pour the grape seed oil on top.

Glaze for 25 minutes in the pre-heated oven.

AGA

Glaze the fish on the bottom of the slow cooking oven.

TIP

Make sure the fish fillets are not too thin; 2.5 centimetres thick is ideal.
Remove the fish from the refrigerator at least an hour in advance so that it can reach room temperature.
Try this recipe also with another fish with a firm structure.

TO SERVE 4

FOR THE TOMATO SAUCE
- 2 shallots, peeled and shredded
- 1 clove garlic, peeled and pressed
- 2 tablespoons olive oil
- 0.5 dl white wine
- 1 chicken stock cube stock
- 400 g tinned chopped tomatoes
- 3 fresh tomatoes, peeled and diced
- 1 teaspoon sambal
- 2 sprigs thyme
- 1 bay leaf
- 80 g tomato paste
- pepper and salt

FOR THE LOBSTER
- 2 raw lobsters, cut lengthwise
- cayenne pepper
- salt
- 12 pearl onions, peeled and stewed
- 200 g scarmoza (= smoked mozzarella), cut into pieces
- 4 sprigs tarragon
- 4 bay leaves

Lobster scarmoza

TOMATO SAUCE

Sauté the shallot and garlic in the olive oil. Deglaze with the white wine.

Add the rest of the ingredients, season with salt and pepper and mix well.

Leave for at least 30 minutes to reduce.

Remove the thyme and bay leaf and mix the sauce until smooth.

Divide the sauce into four individual oven dishes.

LOBSTER

Pre-heat the oven to 200 °C.

Season the lobster with cayenne pepper and salt.

Arrange a piece of lobster in each oven dish and divide the baby onions, scarmoza, tarragon and bay leaf over it.

Bake for 8 minutes in the pre-heated oven.

AGA

Make the sauce on the simmering plate.
Place the oven dishes on the bottom of the roasting oven.

TO SERVE 4

300 g leeks, cleaned and cut into strips
1 + 1 knob of butter
50 g onions, peeled and shredded
800 g mussels, cleaned
pepper
40 g green celery, cleaned and finely chopped
2 sprigs thyme
2 bay leaves
1 dl white wine
2 dl fish fumet
30 g roux
juice of ¼ lemon
0.5 dl cream
150 g Gruyère cheese, grated

Mussels with leek

Sauté the leek in a knob of butter. Reserve.

Sauté the onion in a knob of butter.

Add the mussels and season with salt and pepper.

Add the celery, thyme and bay leaves and moisten with the white wine.

Cook the mussels over a high heat with the lid on and shake regularly until the shells open.

Drain the mussels and collect the cooking liquid. Reserve.

Remove the mussels from the shells.

Boil the mussel juice with the fish stock and add the roux. Boil well and beat into a smooth sauce.

Add the lemon juice and then the cream.

Put the oven on grill setting.

Divide the leeks into four individual greased oven dishes. Divide the mussels over and top with the sauce. Sprinkle with the Gruyère cheese.

Gratinate under the grill until golden brown.

AGA

Sauté the leeks and onion on the simmering plate.
Cook the mussels on the boiling plate.
Make the sauce on the boiling plate.
To gratinate, place as high as possible in the roasting oven.

FOR SIX SARDINES

6 sardines, filleted
zest of ½ lemon
pepper and salt
2 tablespoons wood shavings
pinch of fire herbs
4 sage leaves

Small smoking oven or pan

Smoked sardines

Sprinkle the lemon zest over the sardines and season with salt and pepper.

Spread 2 tablespoons wood shavings over the bottom of the smoker. Add the cherry tomatoes and the sage. Place the drip tray and the smoking rack in the smoker.

Arrange the sardines on the grid.

Slide the oven lid closed, but leave a small opening so that you can see when the smoking process starts.

Heat the oven on high heat. Close the lid as soon as you see the smoke develop. That happens after about 30 seconds.

Reduce the temperature and leave to smoke for 30 minutes.

Turn off the heat and let the sardines rest for a few minutes.

Slide the lid open carefully so that the smoke escapes. Do that under the oven hood.

Serve the smoked sardines hot or cold with a salad.

AGA

Heat the smoker on the boiling plate.
Place the smoker in the slow cooking oven.

TO SERVE 4

2 frozen lobsters, thawed, without shell and cut in half
butter for greasing the individual oven dishes
100 g butter, at room temperature
4 tablespoons fresh green herbs (tarragon, chervil, chives, basil), finely chopped
0.2 dl fish stock
0.5 dl white wine

Lobster with green herbs

Pre-heat the oven to 200 °C.

Pat the lobster meat dry and divide between four individual, buttered oven dishes.

Mix the butter with the herbs.

Cover each piece of lobster with a layer of butter and divide the white wine and the fish stock between the oven dishes.

Bake for 8 minutes in the pre-heated oven.

Serve with a piece of tasty bread.

AGA

Place the oven dishes on the bottom of the roasting oven.

TO SERVE 4

8 plaice fillets
pepper and salt
4 tablespoons ketchup
16 basil leaves
1 orange, washed and sliced
2 heads of red endive, cleaned and leaves separated
2 tomatoes, peeled and diced
olive oil

Plaice with red endive

Pre-heat the oven to 190 °C.

Season the plaice fillets with pepper and salt. Brush the fillets with the ketchup, place 2 basil leaves on top and roll tightly. Secure with a wooden toothpick.

Cover the bottoms of four individual, buttered oven dishes with the orange slices. Divide the red endive over the oven dishes and arrange the plaice rolls on top. Sprinkle the diced tomato on top and drizzle generously with olive oil.

Bake for 8 minutes in the pre-heated oven.

AGA

Place the oven dishes on the bottom of the roasting oven.

TO SERVE 4

4 fillets of plaice	2 tomatoes, peeled, seeded and diced
pepper and salt	4 sprigs thyme
16 basil leaves	500 g clams, rinsed well
4 sun-dried tomatoes	bag of bread croutons
dash of olive oil	
1.5 dl white wine	

Plaice with clams

Pre-heat the oven to 190 °C.

Season the fillets of plaice with pepper and salt. Place 4 basil leaves and a sun-dried tomato on top each time and roll up tightly. Secure with a wooden toothpick.

Place the plaice rolls in an oiled oven dish.

Divide the diced tomato over the oven dish, moisten with the white wine, add the sprigs of thyme and the clams.

Cover the oven dish with aluminium foil.

Steam for 10 minutes in the pre-heated oven.

Serve with the croutons.

AGA

Place the oven dish on the bottom of the roasting oven.

TO SERVE 4

4 redfish fillets, 150 g each	4 sprigs thyme
pepper and salt	4 bay leaves
olive oil	4 spring onions
4 tomatoes, peeled, seeded and quartered	leaves from 1 sprig of tarragon
16 green mini asparagus	flake salt

Redfish with tomato and asparagus

Pre-heat the oven to 150 °C.

Season the redfish fillets with salt and pepper and arrange in individual, oiled oven dishes.

Into each oven dish add four tomato wedges, 4 green asparagus, 1 sprig thyme, a bay leaf and 1 spring onion.

Sprinkle with the tarragon and season with pepper and flake salt. Drizzle richly with olive oil.

Bake for 10 minutes in the pre-heated oven.

AGA

Place the oven dishes on the bottom of the baking oven.

TO SERVE 4
8 fillets of sole
butter for greasing the oven dish
1 shallot, peeled and cut into wedges
pepper and salt

1 dl white wine
3 dl fish fumet
80 g cold butter, cut into small chunks
1 tomato, peeled, seeded and diced

40 g curly parsley, finely chopped

Sole à la dugléré

Pre-heat the oven to 200 °C.

Roll up the sole fillets with the skin on the inside.

Place in a buttered oven dish.

Add the shallot and season with salt and pepper.

Moisten with the white wine and the fish fumet and cover with a buttered baking paper.

Poach for 8 minutes in the pre-heated oven.

Carefully remove the sole rolls from the oven dish and keep hot. Strain the poaching liquid.

Reduce the poaching liquid and dot with the pieces of cold butter.

Finish with the diced tomato and parsley.

AGA

Place the oven dish in the middle of the roasting oven. Make the sauce on the boiling plate.

Haddock rarebit with white cabbage and kale

TO SERVE 4

FOR THE PESTO
40 g kale, cleaned and chopped
1 tablespoon pine nuts
1 clove garlic, peeled and roughly chopped
40 g Parmesan cheese, grated
6 tablespoons olive oil
pepper and salt

FOR THE FISH
360 g kale, cleaned and cut into strips bars
4 tablespoons olive oil
500 g white cabbage, cleaned and cut into strips
4 shallots, peeled and halved lengthways
4 pieces of haddock fillet, 150 g each
pepper and salt
1.25 dl cream
0.5 dl white wine
1 clove garlic, peeled and pressed
40 g grated Parmesan cheese
¼ teaspoon fennel seeds
4 sprigs fresh basil
2 sprigs fresh tarragon

PESTO
Mix all ingredients in a blender into a fine pesto. Season with pepper and salt.

FISH
Pre-heat the oven to 200 °C.

Cook the kale in the olive oil.

Add the white cabbage and shallots and cook for about two minutes.

Scoop everything into an oven dish.

Season the fish with salt and pepper and arrange on top of the vegetables.

Mix the cream, white wine and garlic and pour over the fish.

Drizzle with the pesto.

Sprinkle with the Parmesan cheese and fennel seeds, season with salt and pepper, and add the basil and tarragon.

Bake for 20 minutes in the pre-heated oven.

AGA

Cook the kale on the simmering plate.
Place the oven dish on the bottom of the baking oven.

Lemon sole with turmeric

TO SERVE 4

FOR THE SAUCE
1 dl Noilly Prat
1 dl fish fumet
1 onion, peeled and halved
1 clove garlic, unpeeled
1 celery stalk, cleaned, roughly chopped
1 sprig thyme
1 bay leaf
½ teaspoon turmeric
12 saffron threads
juice of ½ lemon
1 dl cream 40%

FOR THE FISH
1 pointed pepper, seeded and diced
4 lemon sole fillets
pepper and salt
olive oil
½ teaspoon dried chilli flakes
4 tufts tarragon

SAUCE

Bring the Noilly Prat and the fish fumet with the onion, garlic, celery, thyme, bay leaf, turmeric and saffron to the boil and reduce by half.

Strain the juice. Add the lemon juice and then the cream and reduce again.

FISH

Pre-heat the oven to 180 °C.

Blanch the diced paprika very briefly in boiling water. Cool under cold running water and drain.

Season the fish fillets with salt and pepper, fold into three and arrange in four individual, oiled oven dishes.

Add the diced paprika to the sauce and divide between the oven dishes. Season with dried chilli flakes.

Bake for 8 minutes in the pre-heated oven.

Finish with a tuft of tarragon.

AGA

Make the sauce on the boiling plate.
Place the oven dishes on the bottom of the roasting oven.

TO SERVE 4

80 g carrots, cleaned and cut into strips
80 green celery, cleaned and in cut into strips
80 g leeks, cleaned and cut into strips
50 g shredded onion
30 g butter
400 g mussels, cleaned
40 g green celery, cleaned and diced
2 sprigs thyme
2 bay leaves
2 x 1.5 dl white wine
pepper and salt
4 sole fillets, rolled up
160 g skinless salmon fillet, cut into chunks
butter for greasing the oven dish
2.5 dl fish fumet
25 g roux
juice of ¼ lemon
1 dl cream 40%
120 g crayfish tails, pre-cooked
30 g finely chopped chives

Fish waterzooi

Pre-heat the oven to 190 °C.

Blanch the carrots, celery and leek in boiling water for 1 minute. Cool under cold running water and drain. Reserve.

Fry the onion in the butter.

Add the mussels, diced celery, thyme, bay leaf and 1.5 dl white wine and season with salt and pepper.

Cook the mussels over a high heat with the lid on and shake regularly until the shells open.

Drain and collect the mussel liquid.

Remove the mussels from the shells and reserve.

Place the fish in a buttered oven dish. Season with pepper and salt.

Moisten with 1.5 dl white wine and the fish fumet and cover with a buttered baking paper.

Poach for 7 minutes in the pre-heated oven.

Carefully remove the fish from the oven dish and keep hot. Strain the poaching liquid.

Boil the poaching liquid and the mussel juice and add the roux. Boil well and beat into a smooth sauce.

Add the lemon juice and then the cream and boil well.

Add the carrots, celery and leeks.

Place the fish and mussels on the plates and spread the sauce over them. Garnish with the crayfish tails and chives.

AGA

Blanch the vegetables on the boiling plate.
Cook the mussels on the boiling plate.
Place the oven dish on the bottom of the roasting oven.
Make the sauce on the boiling plate.

TO SERVE 4

FOR THE AIOLI
3 egg yolks
2 cloves garlic, peeled and pressed
1 tablespoon vinegar
1 tablespoon lukewarm water
some saffron threads
2 dl olive oil

FOR THE FISH
4 sea bass fillets
pepper and salt
1 courgette, cleaned
½ fennel, cleaned
10 olives, pitted
280 g artichoke hearts in a jar
olive oil

Sea bass with aioli

AIOLI
Place all ingredients in a narrow mixing bowl. Place the hand blender on the bottom of the mixing bowl and mix until you get an emulsion. Now slowly pull the mixer upwards until you get the desired consistency.

FISH
Pre-heat the oven to 190 °C.

Place the sea bass fillets in an oiled oven dish. Season with pepper and salt.

Cut the courgette and fennel into wafer-thin slices with the mandolin slicer.

Arrange the vegetables on top of the fish and add the olives and artichokes.

Drizzle with olive oil and season with pepper and salt.

Bake for 10 minutes in the pre-heated oven.

Serve with toasted bread and the aioli.

AGA

Place the oven dish on the bottom of the roasting oven.

TO SERVE 4

FOR THE FISH
8 fillets of sole, rolled up
pepper and salt
12 sprigs thyme
4 tablespoons dry sherry

FOR THE HOLLANDAISE SAUCE
250 g butter in pieces
50 g of water
1 tablespoon lemon juice
3 egg yolks
pinch of salt
pepper

Sole hollandaise

FISH
Pre-heat the oven to 190 °C.

Place the fish in a buttered oven dish. Season with pepper and salt and add the thyme.

Moisten with sherry and cover with aluminium foil.

Poach for 6 minutes in the pre-heated oven.

HOLLANDAISE SAUCE
Melt the butter and reserve.

Beat the other ingredients in a bain-marie or on a low heat to a frothy emulsion.

Add the melted butter in a trickle, beating constantly.

Serve the sauce with the fish.

AGA

Place the oven dish on the bottom of the roasting oven. Make the sauce on the simmering plate.

TO SERVE 4

1 onion, peeled and shredded
1 clove garlic, peeled and pressed
olive oil
1 apple, peeled, cored and diced
50 g curry powder
1 dl fish fumet
2 dl coconut milk
4 wolffish fillets, 150 g each
pepper and salt
½ lime, finely sliced
½ apple, with skin, without core and diced

Wolffish with curry

Pre-heat the oven to 190 °C.

Cook the onion and garlic in the olive oil.

Add the diced apple and continue to cook.

Add the curry powder, fish fumet and coconut milk and reduce.

Season the wolffish fillets with salt and pepper and arrange in a greased oven dish.

Pour the curry over the fish and add the lime slices.

Bake for 10 minutes in the pre-heated oven.

Garnish with the diced apple.

AGA

Make the curry on the simmering plate.
Place the oven dish in the top of the baking oven.

MEAT & POULTRY

POULTRY | VEAL & BEEF | LAMB | PORK | GAME

Meat and poultry: always something of a party on the table

The hunting season is the perfect time of year to put the tastiest preparations in the oven! One dish that should certainly not be missing here is 'rabbit as mum makes it', a straight flashback to my youth. Also included in this category are spring chicks, coq-au-vin, and pheasant. I'm particularly proud here of my personal variant of the classic vol-au-vent, which I prepare in an earthenware bowl with the puff pastry as a lid. I'm in seventh heaven when my guests poke through the lid and the 'tart' reveals its surprising content!

POULTRY

TO SERVE 4

FOR THE DUCK
2 oven-ready wild ducks
pepper and salt
2 oranges, washed and thickly sliced
2 tablespoons honey
2 bay leaves
2 sprigs thyme
1 sprig of rosemary

FOR THE SAUCE
juice of 2 oranges
50 g Grand Marnier
2 dl poultry stock
dash of soy sauce
50 g cold butter, in little blocks

Canard à l'orange

DUCK

Pre-heat the oven to 180 °C.

Season the ducks inside and out with salt and pepper.

Place a layer of orange slices in a buttered oven dish. Place the ducks on it. Brush the ducks with honey and add the bay leaves and sprigs of thyme and rosemary.

Bake for 60 minutes in the pre-heated oven.

SAUCE

Bring the orange juice with the Grand Marnier, the poultry stock and the soy sauce to the boil and reduce.

Dot with the pieces of cold butter.

Cut the duck and serve with the sauce.

AGA

Place the oven dish on the bottom of the roasting oven. Make the sauce on the boiling plate.

POULTRY

TO SERVE 4

4 slices of smoked bacon, cubed
1 small knob of butter
4 spiced bratwursts
2 onions, peeled and shredded
2 cloves garlic, crushed
3 tablespoons tomato paste
300 g white beans, soaked overnight and drained
800 g tinned tomatoes
1.5 litres of poultry stock
1 dl white wine
pepper and salt
2 sprigs thyme
3 bay leaves
4 cloves
1 teaspoon paprika
1 smoked sausage, cut into chunks
1 duck leg confit

Cassoulet

Pre-heat the oven to 150 °C.

Fry the bacon until crispy in a large stewing pan. Add a knob of butter and fry the sausages.

Remove the bacon and the sausages from the pan and reserve.

Cook the onion and garlic in the same pan and add some extra butter if necessary.

Add the tomato purée and cook together for a while.

Add the soaked beans and the peeled tomatoes and stir.

Moisten with the poultry stock and white wine and season with salt and pepper. Add the thyme, bay leaf, cloves and paprika powder.

Add the smoked sausage and the duck leg confit.

Cook for 2 hours with the lid off in the pre-heated oven. Check regularly whether there is still enough moisture in the pan and add extra poultry stock if necessary.

Add the bacon and sausages and cook for another 30 minutes in the oven. Season with pepper and salt.

AGA

Fry the bacon and sausages on the boiling plate.
Cook the rest on the simmering plate.
Place the stew pot in the slow cooking oven for 3 hours with the lid off.

POULTRY

TO SERVE 4

1 meaty roast chicken, cut into pieces
2 carrots, cleaned and sliced
1 onion, peeled and shredded
2 bay leaves
2 parsley stalks
2 sprigs thyme
1 teaspoon white peppercorns
1 bottle of red wine (Côte du Rhône)
sunflower oil
2 cloves garlic, peeled and pressed
pepper and salt
150 g bacon, cubed
250 g Paris mushrooms
100 g baby onions, peeled
knob of butter
2 tablespoons finely chopped parsley

Coq au vin

Place the chicken, carrots, onion, bay leaf, parsley stems, thyme and peppercorns in a mixing bowl and cover with the red wine. Stir and cover.

Leave to marinate for at least 12 hours in the refrigerator.

Pre-heat the oven to 120 °C.

Remove the chicken from the marinade and pat dry. Strain the marinade and remove the bay leaf, parsley stems, thyme and peppercorns. Set the vegetables and marinade aside.

Fry the chicken pieces all over in the sunflower oil. Add the garlic and vegetables from the marinade and cook for 3 minutes.

Moisten with the strained marinade, season with salt and pepper and bring to the boil.

Cook for 2 hours in the pre-heated oven until tender.

Cook the bacon, mushrooms and baby onions in a knob of butter and add to the coq au vin.

Garnish with the parsley.

AGA

Cook the chicken on the simmering plate.
Cook for at least 2 hours in the simmering oven.
Cook the bacon, mushrooms and sausages on the boiling plate.

POULTRY

TO SERVE 4
FOR THE PIGEONS
4 pigeons, ready to cook
pepper and salt
60 g salted butter
butter for greasing the oven dish

FOR THE PEAS
2 shallots, peeled and shredded
leaves from 1 sprig of tarragon
20 g butter
450 g frozen peas
20 leaves of mint

FOR THE SAUCE
2 sprigs thyme
4 peppercorns
1 bay leaf
0.2 dl cognac
2.5 dl poultry stock
1 dl cream 40%
pepper and salt

Pigeon with peas

PIGEONS
Pre-heat the oven to 180 °C.
Season the pigeons inside and out with salt and pepper.

Let the salted butter become hazelnut brown and fry the pigeons all over in the butter until golden brown.

Place the pigeons in a buttered oven dish. Set the pan with the roasting juice aside.

Bake for 15 to 20 minutes in the pre-heated oven.

PEAS
Start to cook the shallots with the tarragon in the butter. Add the frozen peas and leave to cook for a short while. Add the mint leaves at the last minute.

SAUCE
Place the pan with the pigeons and roasting juice on a high heat. Add the thyme, peppercorns and bay leaf and deglaze with the cognac. Flambé and reduce.

Moisten with the poultry stock and reduce again.

Strain the sauce, add the cream and let it reduce again. Season with pepper and salt.

AGA
Fry the pigeons on the boiling plate.
Place the oven dish on the bottom of the baking oven.
Cook the peas on the boiling plate.

POULTRY

TO SERVE 4

- 2 pheasants, legs cut from the carcass
- pepper and salt
- 1 tablespoon mustard
- 4 cloves
- 3 onions, peeled
- 8 slices of smoked bacon
- 80 + 60 g butter
- 3 sprigs thyme
- 3 bay leaves
- 40 g dash of cognac
- 2.5 dl game stock
- 1 dl cream
- 1 tablespoon cranberries
- juice of ½ lime

Roast pheasant

Pre-heat the oven to 210 °C.

Season the ducks inside and out with salt and pepper and brush all over with the mustard. Prick 2 cloves in 2 onions and stuff one onion in each pheasant.

Wrap each leg in 2 slices of smoked bacon.

Cook 80 grams of butter hazelnut brown in a large stewing pan and bake the pheasants and the legs until golden brown. Add the thyme, bay leaf and the third onion and cover with a lid.

Roast for 30 minutes in the pre-heated oven.

Remove the pheasants from the pan and separate the fillets. Cover with aluminium foil and keep hot.

Cook the legs in a frying pan in 60 grams of butter.

Remove the legs and keep them hot. Pour off the excess fat.

Deglaze the pan with the cognac, game stock and cream and allow to reduce.

Add the cranberries and cook in the mixture for a while.

Refresh with the lime juice.

Serve the pheasant fillets with legs and top with the sauce.

AGA

Fry the pheasants on the boiling plate.
Place the oven dish on the bottom of the roasting oven.
Keep the fillets hot in the warming oven.
Cook the legs on the simmering plate.

POULTRY

TO SERVE 4

FOR THE GLAZE
2 dl ketjap soy sauce
1 tablespoon cranberry jam
2 dl poultry stock

FOR THE DUCK
2 ducks, ready to cook
pepper and salt
50 g butter
2 cloves garlic, unpeeled
4 sprigs thyme

Glazed duck

GLAZE
Boil all ingredients together into a syrup.

DUCK
Pre-heat the oven to 180 °C.

Season the ducks inside and out with salt and pepper.

Heat the butter until hazelnut brown and fry the ducks all over in the butter for 10 minutes.

Place the ducks in an oven dish and pour the cooking fat over it.

Glaze the ducks with the glaze.

Add the garlic and thyme and cover with aluminium foil.

Roast for 20 minutes in the pre-heated oven.

Remove the aluminium foil and roast in the oven for another 10 minutes.

AGA

Make the glaze on the simmering plate.
Lightly fry the ducks on the boiling plate.
Place the oven dish for 3 hours in the simmering oven.

POULTRY

TO SERVE 4

FOR THE PHEASANT AND THE FILLING
3 slices of stale bread without crusts and cut into chunks
1 dl milk
200 g vacuum-packed boiled chestnuts
leaves of 2 sprigs of parsley
1 clove garlic, peeled and pressed
1 egg
2 tablespoons mascarpone
3 tablespoons cognac
3 tablespoons fig jam
2 pheasants, cleaned
pepper
celery salt
1 pinch of d'Espelette allspice
40 g butter, cut into small chunks

FOR THE SAUCE
1 teaspoon cornflour
2 dl cream 40%
2 dl white port
1 sprig of thyme
1 clove garlic, peeled
400 g foie gras
pepper and salt

Stuffed pheasant

PHEASANT AND FILLING

Pre-heat the oven to 160 °C.

Soak the bread in the milk.

Briefly mix the chestnuts, parsley leaves, garlic and squeezed bread in the blender.

Add the egg, mascarpone and cognac and mix again.

Add the fig jam and mix again. Place the filling in a piping bag.

Fill the pheasants with the filling and place on an oven dish. Season with pepper, celery salt and d'Espelette allspice. Place a few pieces of butter on the pheasants. Cover with aluminium foil.

Roast for 1 hour in the pre-heated oven.

SAUCE

Dissolve the cornflour in the cream. Reserve.

Bring the port with the thyme and garlic to the boil and reduce by half.

Add the cream-cornflour mix and reduce again by half.

Add the foie gras and let it dissolve below boiling point. Season with pepper and salt and mix briefly.

AGA

Place the oven dish on the bottom of the baking oven for 1 hour and then transfer to the slow cooking oven for 2 hours.
Make the sauce on the simmering plate.

POULTRY

TO SERVE 4

15 g dried morels
3 slices of stale bread without crusts, cut into chunks
1 dl milk
1 shallot, peeled and shredded
knob of butter
pepper and salt

75 g chicken white (cooked chicken fillet)
75 g boiled ham
125 g chipolata minced meat
20 g pistachio nuts, peeled and finely chopped
1 egg
1 teaspoon veal stock paste

0.2 dl Madeira
1 tablespoon parsley, chopped
30 g duck liver, cut into small cubes
4 guinea fowl fillets
poultry seasoning

Guinea fowl with morels

Soak the dried morels in hot water for several hours. Drain and cut into small pieces.

Pre-heat the oven to 200 °C.

Soak the bread in the milk.

Fry the shallot in a knob of butter.

Add the morels and season with salt and pepper. Reserve.

Mix the chicken white and ham in a blender.

Place in a mixing bowl and add the minced meat, pistachios, egg, veal stock paste, Madeira, parsley, duck liver and stewed morels and mix well with your hands. Season with pepper and salt.

Flatten the guinea fowl fillets on a board under foil.

Season with pepper, salt and poultry seasoning.

Distribute the filling over the guinea fowl fillets and roll up. Season again with salt, pepper and chicken seasoning and roll tightly in aluminium foil.

Place the rolls in an oven dish.

Bake for 35 minutes in the pre-heated oven.

Remove the aluminium foil and cut the rolls into slices.

AGA

Make the filling on the simmering plate.
Cook in the middle of the roasting oven.

POULTRY

TO SERVE 4
FOR THE SPRING CHICKEN
4 spring chickens, ready to cook
pepper
celery salt
200 g butter, at room temperature
1 clove garlic, peeled and pressed
1 teaspoon dried oregano
1 teaspoon dried sage
8 sprigs thyme
butter for greasing the oven dish
a few lumps of butter
16 baby onions, peeled
2 bay leaves

FOR THE SAUCE
2 shallots, peeled and shredded
1 clove garlic, peeled and pressed
30 g butter
300 g forest mushrooms, cleaned and sliced
3 dl veal stock
0.5 dl Noilly Prat or other vermouth
1 dl cream 40%
pepper and salt

Spring chickens with wild mushroom cream sauce

SPRING CHICKENS
Pre-heat the oven to 200 °C.

Season the chickens inside and out with pepper and celery salt.

Mix the butter with the garlic, oregano and sage.

Fill each spring chicken with a quarter of the butter and 2 sprigs of thyme.

Arrange the spring chickens in a buttered oven dish and place a few lumps of butter on top.

Add the baby onions and the bay leaf.

Bake for 25 minutes in the pre-heated oven.

SAUCE
Lightly cook the shallot and garlic in the butter.

Add the forest mushrooms and continue to cook.

Moisten with the veal stock and the Noilly Prat and allow to reduce.
Add the cream and reduce again. Season with pepper and salt.

AGA

Place the oven dish on the bottom of the roasting oven. Make the sauce on the boiling plate.

POULTRY

TO SERVE 4

- 1 kg of pheasant, cut into chunks
- pepper and salt
- 50 g butter
- 2 onions, peeled and roughly chopped
- 2 cloves garlic, peeled and pressed
- 1 large turnip, peeled and diced
- 1 parsnip, peeled and diced
- 250 g mushrooms, trimmed and quartered
- 2 bay leaves
- 3 sprigs thyme
- 2 dl sherry
- 4 dl game stock
- 1 teaspoon Patrelle aroma
- 1 tablespoon flour
- 1 tablespoon Liège syrup
- 2 apples, cored and in wedges
- knob of butter
- 1 tablespoon black sugar
- 0.8 dl cream 40%

Pheasant stew

Pre-heat the oven to 150 °C.

Season the pheasant with salt and pepper and fry in the butter until golden brown all over. Use a large casserole for this. Remove the pheasant from the pan and reserve.

Return the pan to the heat and sauté the onion and garlic.

Add the pheasant, turnip, parsnip, mushrooms, bay leaf and thyme.

Moisten with the sherry and game stock and add the patrelle. Sprinkle with the flour and add the Liège syrup. Cover with a lid.

Cook for 90 minutes in the pre-heated oven until tender.

Stew the apples in a knob of butter and sprinkle with the black sugar. Reserve.

Remove the casserole from the oven and add the apples and cream. Season with pepper and salt.

AGA

Use the boiling plate;
Place the casserole for 3 hours in the simmering oven.

POULTRY

TO SERVE 4
1 chicken
1 litre poultry stock
200 g mushrooms, cleaned and chopped
knob of butter
juice of 1 lemon
pepper and salt
25 g butter
40 g flour
20 meatballs, cooked
30 g finely chopped parsley
1 sheet of puff pastry
1 egg yolk, beaten

Crusty vol-au-vent

Cook the chicken in the poultry stock until tender.

Pre-heat the oven to 200 °C.

Drain the chicken and collect the cooking liquid. Strain the stock and reserve.

Pick the meat from the chicken and cut into small chunks.

Sauté the mushrooms in a knob of butter until cooked. Refresh with the lemon juice and season with pepper and salt.

Melt the butter in a large saucepan and mix in the flour well. Leave the roux to dry. Add the strained chicken stock and the cooking liquid from the mushrooms, stirring all the time. Bring to the boil quickly and stir vigorously until you get a smooth sauce. Season with pepper and salt.

Add the mushrooms, meatballs and parsley.

Place the filling in a round oven dish and cover with the puff pastry. Press the edges well and brush the puff pastry with the egg yolk.

Bake for 20 minutes in the pre-heated oven.

AGA

Boil the chicken on the simmering plate.
Place the oven dish on the bottom of the roasting oven.

POULTRY

TO SERVE 6

FOR THE CRANBERRY SAUCE
340 g cranberries
250 g orange juice
150 g sugar

FOR THE SPICE MIX
1 tablespoon fine salt
1 tablespoon onion powder
1 teaspoon garlic powder
1 teaspoon coriander powder
½ teaspoon cayenne pepper
¼ teaspoon clove powder
1 teaspoon ground pepper
1 teaspoon celery salt
1 teaspoon ginger powder
1 tablespoon paprika
1 teaspoon cumin powder

FOR THE MEATBALLS
1 kg minced chicken
2 shallots, peeled and shredded
2 tablespoons breadcrumbs
30 g butter

FOR THE CREAM SAUCE:
4 dl veal stock
dash of cognac
3 dl cream 40%
pepper and salt

Swedish meatballs

Pre-heat the oven to 180 °C.

Bring the cranberries, orange juice and sugar to the boil and reduce over low heat until the berries burst. Leave to simmer for a further 5 minutes. Leave to cool completely.

Mix all the ingredients for the meat balls. Store in a closed box or jar.

Mix the minced chicken, shallot, breadcrumbs and 2 tablespoons the spice mix with the food processor or with your hands.

Roll out balls of 3 centimetres in diameter.

Fry the balls in the butter until brown all over and place them in an oven dish.

Bring the veal stock and cognac to the boil and reduce by half.

Mix in the cream, season with salt and pepper and pour over the meatballs.

Bake for 20 minutes in the pre-heated oven.

Serve with a spoonful of cranberry sauce.

AGA

Make the cranberry sauce on the simmering plate.
Fry the meatballs on the boiling plate.
Cook the stock on the boiling plate.
Place the oven dish in the centre of the baking oven.

VEAL & BEEF

TO SERVE 6

- 1200 g beef from the neck or shoulder, roughly chopped
- 3 onions, peeled and roughly chopped
- 2 cloves garlic, peeled and pressed
- 1 large carrot, cleaned and roughly chopped
- 2 celery stalks, cleaned and roughly chopped
- 3 bay leaves
- 4 sprigs thyme
- 8 sage leaves
- 2 cloves
- 5 juniper berries
- 5 dl red wine (Burgundy)
- 50 g butter
- 200 g fresh bacon, cut into strips
- pepper and salt
- 250 g Parisian mushrooms, cleaned and quartered
- 2 level tablespoons flour
- 2.5 dl veal stock

Boeuf bourguignon

Place the meat, onion, garlic, carrot, celery, bay leaf, thyme, sage, juniper berries and cloves in a mixing bowl and cover with the red wine. Stir and cover.

Leave to marinate for at least 12 hours in the refrigerator.

Pre-heat the oven to 160 °C.

Remove the meat from the marinade. Strain the marinade and remove the bay leaf, thyme, sage, cloves and juniper berries. Set the vegetables and marinade aside.

Heat the butter till hazelnut brown in the casserole and lightly fry the bacon.

Add the beef and brown all over. Season with pepper and salt.

Add the mushrooms and cook together for a while.

Add the vegetables from the marinade and let everything cook together for a while.

Sprinkle with the flour and stir.

Moisten with the strained marinade and the veal stock. Stir well again and cover with a lid.

Stew for 90 minutes in the pre-heated oven, stirring occasionally to prevent sticking.

AGA

Use the boiling plate;
Place the stew pot in the slow cooking oven for 2 hours with the with lid on.

VEAL & BEEF

TO SERVE 4
1 rack of veal, with legs cleaned
flake salt
steak pepper
4 sprigs tarragon
4 sprigs thyme
2 sprigs rosemary
60 g butter, cut into small chunks
1 garlic bulb, halved
2 bay leaves

Roasted veal crown

Pre-heat the oven to 160 °C.

Wrap aluminium foil around the legs to protect them.

Place the rack of veal in an oven dish. Season with flaky salt and steak pepper.

Add the tarragon, thyme and rosemary. Place the pieces of butter on top of the meat and arrange the garlic and bay leaf on top.

Bake for 35 minutes in the pre-heated oven.

Regularly spoon the run-off fat back over the meat.

AGA

Place the oven dish on the bottom of the baking oven.

VEAL & BEEF

TO SERVE 6

200 g pearl onions, peeled
25 + 25 g butter
1.5 litres white stock
pepper and salt
300 g Paris mushrooms, cleaned and quartered
juice of ½ lemon
250 g minced veal

1.5 kg of veal from the shoulder and neck, cut into equal pieces
2 cloves
2 onions, peeled
1 carrot, cleaned
4 sprigs curly parsley
1 piece of leek white, 6 cm

4 parsley stalks
2 bay leaves
3 sprigs thyme
30 g butter
40 g flour
pinch of nutmeg
a few drops of lemon juice
2 dl cream

Blanquette of veal

Pre-heat the oven to 140 °C.

Lightly fry the baby onions in 25 grams of butter. Moisten with 1 dl of white stock and season with salt and pepper. Cover with a lid and leave to stew for 15 minutes. Reserve.

Lightly fry the mushrooms in 25 grams of butter. Moisten with 1 dl of white stock, add the lemon juice and season with salt and pepper. Cover with a lid and stew until cooked.

Drain the mushrooms and collect the cooking liquid. Reserve.

Season the veal mince with salt and pepper and roll into balls. Boil in water until they float to the top. Drain and Reserve.

Bring the rest of the white stock to the boil and add the veal.

Pierce a clove into each onion and add.

Tie the carrot, curly parsley, leek, parsley stems, bay leaf and thyme together and add. Cover with a lid.

Cook in the pre-heated oven for 1 hour, skimming regularly.

Remove the meat from the stock. Reserve.

Melt the butter in a large saucepan and mix in the flour well. Leave the roux to dry. Add the strained stock and the cooking liquid from the mushrooms, stirring all the time. Bring quickly to the boil and stir vigorously until you get a smooth sauce. Season with nutmeg, refresh with a few drops of lemon juice and add the cream.

Add the meat, mushrooms and baby onions and let it return to the boil.

AGA

Fry the baby onions on the simmering plate and cook them in the simmering oven or slow cooking oven without browning.
Fry the mushrooms on the simmering plate.
Boil the meatballs on the boiling plate.

TIP

Soak the baby onions briefly in hot water. This makes them easier to peel.

VEAL & BEEF

TO SERVE 4

FOR THE GREMOLATA
leaves of ½ a bunch of flat parsley, finely chopped
2 cloves garlic, peeled and shredded
zest of 1 lemon

FOR THE OSSOBUCCO
4 veal shanks
pepper and salt
4 tablespoons flour
40 g olive oil
4 carrots, cleaned and sliced
2 large onions, peeled and sliced
4 stalks of celery, cleaned and cut into strips
5 San Marzano tomatoes, roughly chopped
1 tablespoon veal stock paste
3 dl red port
1 dl orange juice
4 bay leaves
4 sprigs thyme
2 sprigs rosemary
2 cloves garlic
5 dl passata

Ossobuco

GREMOLATA
Mix the flat parsley, garlic and lemon zest. Keep cool.

OSSOBUCCO
Pre-heat the oven to 120 °C.

Season the veal shanks with salt and pepper and mix in the flour. Knock off the excess flour.

Fry the shanks brown on both sides in the olive oil and arrange them in a deep oven dish.

Add some olive oil in the same pan and sauté the carrots, onion and celery. Add the tomatoes and veal stock paste, moisten with the port and orange juice and stir.

Add the bay leaf, thyme, rosemary and garlic and stir.

Spoon the stewed vegetables over the shanks in the oven dish and pour in all the liquid.

Cover with the passata and make sure that the shanks are completely covered. Add extra passata or water if necessary.

Cook for 3 hours in the pre-heated oven.

Serve the ossobuco with the gremolata and place a spoon in the marrow.

AGA

Fry the shanks on the boiling plate.
Fry everything on the simmering plate.
Place the oven dish in the simmering oven

TIP

The flour on the shanks creates a thick sauce.
The veal stock paste can be replaced by a beef stock cube.

LAMB

TO SERVE 4
1 leg of lamb, 1.5 kg
5 cloves garlic, peeled and halved
olive oil
pepper and salt
12 sprigs thyme
4 shallots, peeled and halved
12 figs, in wedges
5 tablespoons olive oil
1 tablespoon honey

Leg of lamb with figs

Pre-heat the oven to 200 °C.

Score the leg of lamb here and there with a sharp knife and press the garlic cloves into the meat.

Rub the leg with the olive oil and season with salt and pepper.

Arrange the leg of lamb in an oiled oven dish and add the sprigs of thyme.

Roast for 15 minutes in the pre-heated oven.

Remove the oven dish from the oven and lower the temperature to 180 °C.

Add the shallots.

Cook the leg of lamb for one hour in the oven until tender.

Drizzle the figs with the olive oil and honey and add them to the leg of lamb after 55 minutes.

AGA

Roast for the leg of lamb in the middle of the roasting oven.
Cook the leg on the bottom of the baking oven.

LAMB

TO SERVE 4

FOR THE HERB CRUST
25 g panko breadcrumbs
2 cloves garlic, peeled
leaves of 1 bunch of flat parsley
needles from 1 sprig of rosemary
20 leaves of mint
zest of 1 lime
1 egg yolk

FOR THE SADDLE OF LAMB
1 saddle of lamb
pepper and salt
4 tablespoons olive oil
3 onions, peeled and sliced
3 cloves garlic, with skin
2 sprigs rosemary
1 lime, washed and finely sliced
2 tablespoons colza oil

Saddle of lamb with herb crust

HERB CRUST
Mix all ingredients into a paste in the blender.

SADDLE OF LAMB
Pre-heat the oven to 120 °C.

Season the saddle with salt and pepper and fry in the olive oil until brown all over.

Place the onion, garlic, rosemary and lime slices in a layer in a roasting tin and drizzle with the colza oil.

Arrange the saddle of lamb on top and brush with the herb crust.

Bake for 2 hours in the pre-heated oven.

AGA

Fry the saddle of lamb on the boiling plate.
Bake the saddle of lamb in the simmering oven.

LAMB

TO SERVE 6

- 1.2 kg lamb stewing meat
- 2 onions, peeled and roughly chopped
- 1 large carrot, cleaned and roughly chopped
- 3 cloves garlic, peeled and pressed
- 3 bay leaves
- 4 sprigs thyme
- 2 sprigs rosemary
- 4 sprigs oregano
- 6 leaves of sage
- 1 bottle of red wine
- pepper and salt
- 4 tablespoons olive oil
- 2 tablespoons flour
- 1 tablespoon concentrated tomato paste
- 1 tablespoon mustard
- 350 g waxy potatoes, peeled and cut into chunks
- 240 g peeled tomatoes
- 5 dl lamb stock

Lamb daube

Place the meat, onion, carrot, garlic, bay leaf, thyme, rosemary, oregano and sage in a mixing bowl and cover with the red wine. Stir and cover.

Leave to marinate for at least 12 hours in the refrigerator.

Pre-heat the oven to 150 °C.

Remove the meat from the marinade. Strain the marinade and remove the bay leaf, thyme, rosemary, oregano and sage leaves. Set the vegetables and marinade aside.

Season the meat with pepper and salt.

Fry the meat in the olive oil in a large casserole until brown.

Sprinkle with the flour. Add the tomato purée, mustard, potatoes, peeled tomatoes and vegetables from the marinade and moisten with the lamb stock and the marinade.

Stir well and bring to the boil. Cover with a lid.

Stew for 2 hours in the pre-heated oven, stirring occasionally to prevent sticking.

AGA

Lightly fry the meat on the boiling plate.
Place the stew pot in the slow cooking oven for 3 hours with the lid on.

LAMB

Moussaka

TO SERVE 6

- 3 medium onions, peeled and shredded
- 2 cloves garlic, peeled and pressed
- olive oil
- 3 carrots, cleaned and diced
- 3 stalks of celery, cleaned and diced
- pepper and salt
- 1 kg of minced lamb
- 120 g tomato paste
- pinch of harissa
- 4 dl red wine
- 400 g passata
- 1 teaspoon dried oregano
- ½ teaspoon cumin powder
- ½ teaspoon cinnamon powder
- 30 g butter
- 40 g flour
- 7 dl milk
- 750 g potatoes, peeled
- 2 courgettes, with skin
- 250 g mozzarella, grated
- 50 g Parmesan cheese, finely grated
- 2 pieces of pecorino with crust

Pre-heat the oven to 160 °C.

Fry the onion and garlic in 4 tablespoons olive oil in a large casserole.

Add the carrots and the celery and leave to cook for 10 minutes. Season with pepper and salt.

Fry the minced lamb loose and crispy in 4 tablespoons olive oil.

Add the baked meat to the vegetables. Add the tomato purée, harissa, red wine, passata, oregano, cumin and cinnamon and season with salt and pepper. Stir and cover with a lid.

Cook for 1 hour in the pre-heated oven.

Melt the butter in a large saucepan and mix in the flour well. Leave the roux to dry. Add the milk while stirring. Bring quickly to the boil and stir vigorously until you get a smooth sauce.

Cut the potatoes and courgette into fine slices with a mandolin slicer.

Remove the casserole from the oven.

Increase the oven temperature to 180 ° C.

Spoon a layer of béchamel sauce into an oiled deep oven dish.

Then arrange the potatoes slices on the sauce and season with salt and pepper.

Follow with a layer of courgette slices.

Spoon over a layer of the minced lamb and flatten.

Repeat until everything is used up.

Finish with a layer of béchamel sauce and sprinkle with the mozzarella and Parmesan cheese. Press the pecorino pieces crust side up into the moussaka.

Bake the moussaka for 40 minutes in the pre-heated oven.

AGA

Fry the onion on the simmering plate
Fry the minced meat on the simmering plate.
Stew the vegetables and meat in the simmering oven.
Make the soup on the boiling plate.
Bake the moussaka in the baking oven.

LAMB

TO SERVE 4
FOR THE LEG OF LAMB
1 leg of lamb
5 cloves garlic, peeled and sliced
2 tablespoons olive oil
2 tablespoons mustard
leaves of 10 sprigs of thyme
needles from 10 sprigs of rosemary, finely chopped
pepper and salt
2 bay leaves
60 g butter

FOR THE MINT SAUCE
0.5 dl white wine vinegar
2 shallots, peeled and shredded
20 mint leaves, finely chopped
4 egg yolks
300 g cold butter, cut into small chunks
pepper and salt
8 mint leaves

Slow-cooked leg of lamb with mint

LEG OF LAMB
Pre-heat the oven to 60 °C.

Make some notches in the meat with a sharp knife and press slices of garlic into them.

Brush the leg of lamb with the oil and cover with the mustard, thyme and rosemary. Season with pepper and salt and place the bay leaves on top.

Place a grille in a roasting pan and arrange the leg of lamb on top.

Cook for least 9 hours in the pre-heated oven until tender.

Remove the leg of lamb from the oven.

Pre-heat the oven to 240 °C.

Spread the butter over the leg of lamb and roast in the pre-heated oven until a core temperature of 63 °C is reached.

Remove the leg of lamb from the oven and keep hot.

MINT SAUCE
Bring the white wine vinegar to the boil along with the shallot and finely chopped mint, and reduce to 3 tablespoons liquid.

Reduce the heat and add the egg yolks one at a time, beating constantly. Make sure the sauce does not boil.

Fold in the chunks of butter, beating constantly.

Season with salt and pepper and finish with the mint leaves.

AGA

Place the roasting pan in the slow cooking oven.
Roast the leg of lamb in the roasting oven until a core temperature of 63 ° C is reached.
Reduce the white wine vinegar on the boiling plate.
Make the sauce on the simmering plate.

TIP

The leg of lamb can safely cook in the oven for more than 9 hours.
Add a dash of cream or a little cornflour if the sauce curdles.
You can make the sauce in advance and keep it hot in a thermos.

PORK

FOR 10 MEATBALLS
1 kg mixed minced pork/beef
1 egg
2 teaspoons dried oregano
1 teaspoon dried thyme
70 g breadcrumbs
pepper and salt
30 + 30 g butter
2 shallots, peeled and roughly chopped
2 cloves garlic, peeled and pressed
2 carrots, cleaned and roughly chopped
350 g butternut squash, roughly chopped
250 g oyster mushrooms, brushed clean
1 dl white wine
2 dl poultry stock
400 g canned tomato pulp
20 cherry tomatoes
3 bay leaves
200 g spinach, washed

Meatballs with pumpkin and oyster mushrooms

Pre-heat the oven to 120 °C.

Mix the minced meat, egg, oregano, thyme and breadcrumbs with the food processor or with your hands and season with salt and pepper.

Roll out 10 balls.

Fry the meatballs on a high heat in 30 grams of butter until golden brown.

Place the meatballs in an oven dish.

Lightly cook the shallot and garlic in 30 grams of butter. Add the carrots and the butternut squash and cook for 5 minutes. Add the oyster mushrooms and allow to cook for another 5 minutes.

Moisten with the white wine and the poultry stock. Add the tomato pulp, cherry tomatoes the bay leaves. Season with salt and pepper and bring to the boil.

Mix in the spinach, season with salt and pepper and pour over the meatballs in the oven dish.

Cook for 1 hour in the pre-heated oven.

AGA

Fry the meatballs and vegetables on the boiling plate. Place the oven dish in the slow cooking oven.

TIP

Serve with sweet potato purée.

PORK

TO SERVE 6

1.5 kg minced meat
3 egg yolks
2 shallots, peeled and shredded
1 clove garlic, peeled and shredded
3 tablespoons breadcrumbs
50 g mustard
40 g tomato ketchup
½ bunch of flat parsley, finely chopped
pepper and salt
20 g butter for greasing the mould
250 g thin slices of smoked ham with the rind removed
8 eggs, hard boiled and peeled
4 sprigs oregano

Minced bread with hidden eggs

Pre-heat the oven to 200 °C.

Mix the minced meat, egg yolks, shallot, garlic, breadcrumbs, mustard, tomato ketchup and parsley with the food processor or with your hands and season with salt and pepper.

Cover a buttered silicone turban mould with the smoked ham.

Place two-thirds of the minced meat mixture in the tin. Arrange the hard-boiled eggs on top and press into the minced meat. Cover with the remaining mince and press well. Fold the overhanging pieces of ham over the minced meat.

Bake for 30 minutes in the pre-heated oven.

Remove from the mould and garnish with the sprigs of oregano.

AGA

Place the mould on the bottom of the roasting oven.

PORK

TO SERVE 4
2 tablespoons mustard
6 tablespoons sweet soy sauce
1 tablespoon paprika
1 teaspoon smoked paprika
50 g brown sugar
2 cloves garlic, peeled
2 onions, peeled and roughly chopped
1 kg pork belly

Roast belly pork

Mix the mustard, soy sauce, paprika, brown sugar, garlic and onions in a blender to a smooth sauce.

Brush the belly pork all over with the sauce and leave to marinate, covered, in the refrigerator for 24 hours.

Pre-heat the oven to 210 °C.

Place a sheet of baking paper on a rack and arrange the belly pork on top.

Roast for 50 minutes in the pre-heated oven.

AGA

Place the belly pork on a grill plate and roast for 50 minutes in the roasting oven.

PORK

TO SERVE 4
1 tablespoon brown sugar
1 tablespoon tomato paste
2 cloves garlic, peeled and shredded
¼ teaspoon ginger powder
½ teaspoon coriander seeds
½ teaspoon d'Espelette allspice
2 dl Ricard
pepper and sea salt
2 belly ribs

Glazed belly ribs

Mix the sugar, tomato purée, garlic, ginger powder, coriander seeds, d'Espelette allspice and Ricard and season with pepper and sea salt. Turn the belly ribs in this marinade and leave to marinate for 12 hours in the refrigerator.

Pre-heat the oven to 90 °C.

Place a sheet of baking paper in a baking roasting pan and place a rack on top.

Place the ribs on the rack and bake for 8 hours in the pre-heated oven.

Pour the marinade into a small pan and put it in the oven to thicken.

After 8 hours, remove the ribs from the oven, coat with the thickened marinade and place back on the rack in the roasting tray.

Pre-heat the oven to 250 °C.

Bake in the roasting oven until the edges turn black.

AGA

Bake the belly ribs for 8 hours in the simmering oven. After that, bake in the roasting oven until the edges turn black.

TIP

Belly ribs contain more meat and are popularly referred to as 'fatty ribs'.

PORK

Italian minced meat dish

TO SERVE 4

- 1 onion, peeled and shredded
- 2 cloves garlic, peeled and pressed
- 2 tablespoons olive oil
- 500 g mixed minced meat, pork/veal
- 2 celery stalks, sliced
- 250 g mushrooms, trimmed and sliced
- 140 g tomato paste
- needles of ½ sprig of rosemary, finely chopped
- 1.5 dl red wine
- 700 g potatoes, peeled and cut into wafer-thin slices, slightly pre-cooked
- 250 g camembert
- 8 basil leaves

Pre-heat the oven to 200 °C.

Fry the onion and garlic in the olive oil.

Add the minced meat, celery and mushrooms and leave to cook.

Add the tomato paste, rosemary and red wine. Mix well and leave to cook.

Place in a buttered oven dish and top with the slices of potato. Spread the camembert over it.

Bake for 25 minutes in the pre-heated oven.

Garnish with a few basil leaves.

AGA

Fry everything on the simmering plate.
Place the oven dish on the bottom of the roasting oven.

PORK

TO SERVE 4

- 1 cauliflower, without leaves
- 20 g butter
- 500 g minced pork
- 1 egg yolk
- ½ pointed pepper, very finely chopped
- 1 shallot, peeled and shredded
- pinch of nutmeg
- pinch of cayenne pepper
- pepper and salt
- 8 slices of processed cheddar cheese
- 1 teaspoon chimichurri

Stuffed cauliflower

Pre-heat the oven to 180 °C.

Bring a large pot of well-salted water to the boil.

Carefully immerse the cauliflower into it and cook for 3 minutes.

Drain, place in a buttered oven dish and leave to cool.

Mix the minced meat, egg yolk, pointed pepper, shallot, nutmeg and cayenne pepper with the food processor or with your hands and season with salt and pepper.

Remove a few florets from the cauliflower here and there with a spoon.

Roll the minced meat into balls and fill the gaps with it.

Top with the cheddar slices and sprinkle with the chimichurri.

Roast for 20 minutes in the pre-heated oven.

AGA

Boil the cauliflower on the boiling plate.
Place the oven dish in the baking oven.

PORK

FOR A 1.5 L PATE MOULD
250 g belly pork
250 g lean pork
125 g chicken livers
1 onion, peeled and shredded
1 clove garlic, peeled and pressed
20 g butter
2 dl veal stock
2 teaspoons mixed herbs (pepper, salt, nutmeg, mace and cloves)
dash of cognac
75 g pistachios, peeled
30 slices of smoked bacon

Paté with pistachios

Run the belly pork, pork and chicken livers through the meat grinder or ask the butcher to do so.

Sauté the kale and garlic in the butter. Add the veal stock and bring to the boil.

Reduce to a third and leave to cool.

Pre-heat the oven to 170 °C.

Mix the meat, mixed herbs, cognac, reduced veal stock and pistachios with the food processor or with your hands.

Line a pâté tin or terrine with the bacon slices and let the bacon hang over the sides.

Pour the meat mixture into the terrine and fold the bacon nicely over to close.

Cover the mould or terrine with a lid or with aluminium foil.

Place the mould in a roasting tin in 2 centimetres of boiling water.

Bake for 50 minutes in the bain-marie in the pre-heated oven.

Leave to cool with a weight on it.

AGA

Cook the meat stock on the boiling plate.
Bake the pâté on the bottom of the baking oven.

PORK

TO SERVE 4

- 2 shallots, peeled and shredded
- 1 clove garlic, peeled and shredded
- 30 + 50 g butter
- 3 tablespoons breadcrumbs
- 2 tablespoons parsley, finely chopped
- 6 sage leaves, finely chopped
- pepper and salt
- pinch of nutmeg
- 1 kg minced pork
- 150 g smoked sausage, without skin and cut into 0.5 cm cubes
- 1 egg yolk
- 100 g Parmesan cheese, grated

Meatloaf

Pre-heat the oven to 200 °C.

Sauté the shallot and garlic in 30 grams of butter.

Add the breadcrumbs, parsley and sage, season with salt, pepper and nutmeg and simmer for a while.

Mix the minced meat, smoked sausage, egg yolk, Parmesan cheese and stewed mixture with the food processor or with your hands.

Form a meat bun and arrange in an oven dish.

Melt 50 grams of butter and pour over the meat bun.

Bake for 30 minutes in the pre-heated oven.

Reduce the temperature to 160 °C and bake for another 30 minutes.

AGA

Fry everything on the simmering plate.
Place the oven dish on the bottom of the roasting oven.
Transfer the oven dish to the baking oven.

PORK

FOR 4 SAUSAGE ROLLS
250 g mixed minced meat
1 egg + 1 egg, beaten
1 teaspoon mustard
1 teaspoon soy sauce
1 tablespoon breadcrumbs
pepper and salt
nutmeg
1 square sheet of puff pastry, quartered

Sausage rolls

Pre-heat the oven to 200 °C.

Mix the minced meat, egg, mustard, ketchup and breadcrumbs with the food processor or with your hands and season with pepper, salt and nutmeg.

Divide the minced meat into four portions. Roll it into sausages.

Place a roll of minced meat mixture in the centre of each piece of dough.

Fold the dough and brush with the beaten egg.

Bake for 20 minutes in the pre-heated oven.

AGA

Bake on the bottom of the roasting oven.

PORK

TO SERVE 4

750 g mixed minced meat, pork/veal	40 g flour
30 + 30 + 30 g butter	7 dl milk
1 kg Belgian endive, cleaned and roughly chopped	juice of ½ lemon
	nutmeg
pepper and salt	250 g Emmental cheese, finely grated

Belgian endive dish with minced meat

Pre-heat the oven to 180 °C.

Fry the minced meat till brown in 30 grams of butter.

Season the Belgian endive with salt and pepper and simmer, with the lid on, in 30 grams of butter.

Drain the Belgian endive and collect the cooking liquid.

Melt 30 grams of butter in a large saucepan and mix in the flour well. Leave the roux to dry. Add the milk and 0.5 dl of the cooking liquid while stirring. Bring quickly to the boil and stir vigorously until you get a smooth sauce.

Refresh with the lemon juice and season with pepper, salt and nutmeg.

Remove the pan from the heat and add 100 grams of grated Emmental cheese. Stir well until all the cheese has melted.

Transfer the minced meat into a greased oven dish. Spoon the Belgian endive on top and pour the sauce over it.

Sprinkle with the rest of the grated cheese.

Bake for 20 minutes in the pre-heated oven.

Put the oven on grill setting and leave the cheese for a while to crust under the grill.

AGA

Fry the minced meat on the boiling plate.
Fry the Belgian endive on the simmering plate.
Make the sauce on the boiling plate.
Place the oven dish on the bottom of the roasting oven.
Place the oven dish as high as possible in the roasting oven in order to crust the cheese.

GAME

Hare paté

FOR ONE 5-LITRE PATE MOULD OR TWO 2.5 LITRE MOULDS

- 1 kg hare, cut into chunks
- 1 kg of pork liver, cut into chunks
- 2 kg neck of pork, cut into blocks
- pepper and salt
- ¾ litre red wine
- 2 onions, peeled and shredded
- 3 bay leaves
- 3 sprigs thyme
- 2 sprigs parsley
- 30 g butter
- 15 g salt
- 6 g pepper
- 30 slices of smoked bacon

Place all the pieces of meat in a large bowl, season with salt and pepper and pour over the red wine. Add the onion, the bay leaf, thyme and parsley. Stir and cover.

Leave to marinate for at least 12 hours.

Remove the meat from the marinade. Strain the marinade and remove the bay leaf, thyme and parsley.

Sauté the onion in the butter

Mince the meat through the meat grinder and mix with the fried onion, salt and pepper.

Leave to rest for at least 12 hours in the refrigerator.

Pre-heat the oven to 180 °C.

Line a pâté tin or a terrine with the bacon slices and let the bacon hang over the edge.

Turn the meat mixture into the terrine and fold it nicely closed with the bacon.

Cover the mould or terrine with a lid or with aluminium foil.

Place the tin in a roasting tin in 2 centimetres of boiling water.

Bake for 1 hour in the pre-heated oven.

Leave to cool with a weight on it.

AGA

Bake the pâté for 90 minutes in the bain-marie in the slow cooking oven.

TIP

Cut the meat small enough to pass through the meat grinder.

GAME

TO SERVE 4

1 rabbit, cut into chunks
pepper and salt
50 g butter
2 large onions, peeled and halved
2 carrots, cleaned and roughly chopped
2 tablespoons flour
2 bottles of Rodenbach beer
2 tablespoons mustard
3 bay leaves
2 sprigs thyme
2 cloves

Rabbit as mum makes it

Pre-heat the oven to 150 °C.

Season the rabbit with salt and pepper and fry in the butter until golden brown.

Add the onion and the carrots.

Sprinkle with the flour.

Moisten with the Rodenbach.

Add the mustard, bay leaf, thyme and clove and season with salt and pepper. Cover with the lid.

Roast for 2 hours in the pre-heated oven.

AGA

Place the casserole for 2.5 hours in the slow cooking oven.

GAME

Hare stew

TO SERVE 4
60 g butter
1 hare, trimmed and cut into sections
pepper and salt
2 large onions, peeled and sliced
3 bay leaves
3 sprigs thyme
3 tablespoons flour
1 bottle of red wine
1 tablespoon game stock (paste)
2 slices of gingerbread
2 tablespoons mustard
50 g dark chocolate, broken into pieces

Pre-heat the oven to 100 °C.

Heat the butter till hazelnut brown in a casserole and lightly fry the sections of hare until brown all over. Season with pepper and salt.

Add the onion, the bay leaves and the thyme and cook for 5 minutes.

Sprinkle the flour over the meat and moisten with red wine until the hare is almost completely covered.

Bring to the boil and add the gingerbread, mustard and chocolate.

Cook for 3 hours with the lid off in the pre-heated oven.

AGA

Brown the hare on the boiling plate.
Place the casserole, uncovered, for 3 hours in the slow cooking oven.

GAME

Young venison ragout

TO SERVE 4

5 dl water
500 g sugar
300 g purple carrots, cleaned
50 g butter
800 g young venison, cut into chunks
pepper and salt
1 tablespoon flour
2 dl red port
2.2 dl brown veal stock
1 tablespoon brown sugar
2 onions, peeled and sliced
200 g pumpkin cubes
1 tablespoon mustard
1 sprig of rosemary
2 sprigs thyme
2 bay leaves

Pre-heat the oven to 150 °C.

Make a sugar syrup with the water and sugar and let the carrots simmer in this until they are cooked. Reserve.

Heat the butter till hazelnut brown in a casserole and lightly fry the chunks of venison until brown all over. Season with salt and pepper and sprinkle with the flour.

Deglaze with the port vinegar and the veal stock. Add the sugar, onion, pumpkin, mustard, rosemary, thyme and bay leaf and stir well. Close the pan with a lid.

Cook for 90 minutes in the pre-heated oven. Stir regularly.

Heat the glazed carrots and serve them with the ragout.

AGA

Glaze the carrots on the simmering plate.
Lightly brown the venison on the boiling plate.
Place the casserole for 2 hours in the simmering oven.
Heat the carrots on the simmering plate.

DESSERTS

Desserts: sweet, but not a sin

For the sweet-tooths among us, the dessert is without a doubt the highlight of the meal. If we allow ourselves a truly indulgent meal, this is also the proverbial icing on the cake - and the perfect ending. Nor does preparing a delicious dessert have to be unnecessarily complicated. Here too we play mainly on originality, delicious textures and pure flavours.

FOR 20 MINI PAVLOVAS

FOR THE MERINGUE:
250 g egg white
pinch of salt
310 g granulated sugar
310 g icing sugar
30 g cornflour

FOR THE MOUSSE:
2 eggs
100 g icing sugar
10 g vanilla sugar
500 g mascarpone

FOR THE CRANBERRIES:
340 g fresh cranberries
100 g granulated sugar
juice of ½ lime

Meringue with fresh cranberries

MERINGUE
Pre-heat the oven to 90 °C.

Place the egg whites in a clean, dry and fat-free mixing bowl of the food processor. Beat the egg whites with the pinch of salt into a frothy mass.

Continue to run the food processor with the whisk and add the granulated sugar spoon by spoon. Check whether the sugar has been completely absorbed. That will take at least 8 minutes.

Now continue to beat until the foam forms firm peaks.

Fold the icing sugar and cornflour carefully and in parts into the beaten egg whites.

Place a sheet of baking paper or a baking mat on a baking tray.

Spoon heaps of egg white side by side on the baking tray and make a hollow in the middle to fill with the mousse.

Bake for 90 minutes in the pre-heated oven. Leave on a wire rack to cool

MOUSSE
Split the eggs and place the yolks in the mixing bowl of a food processor. Add the icing sugar and vanilla sugar and beat into a light yellow mass.

Add the mascarpone and let the machine run for a while. Transfer into another bowl.

Clean the mixing bowl thoroughly and beat the egg whites until stiff.

Fold the egg whites gently into the mascarpone mixture.

Fry the fresh cranberries briefly with the sugar and lime juice. Add half of this to the mascarpone mixture.

Spoon the mousse into the cavities of the cooled meringues and finish with the rest of the stewed cranberries.

AGA

Bake the meringue in the centre of the
slow cooking oven.
Fry the cranberries on the simmering plate.

TO SERVE 8

FOR THE CARAMEL
0.5 dl cold water
200 g granulated sugar
1.5 dl hot water

FOR THE CREAM:
3 eggs
4 egg yolks
125 + 100 g granulated sugar
7.5 dl whole milk
contents of 1 vanilla pod

Crème caramel

CARAMEL

Fill a large roasting tin with cold water and arrange 8 ramekins in it.

Put the cold water in a saucepan and add the sugar. Bring this to the boil without stirring and let it caramelize until you get a golden brown colour. Immediately remove from the heat and carefully deglaze with the hot water. Boil again and let the caramel reduce a little.

Quickly pour the caramel into the ramekins and leave to cool.

CREAM

Pre-heat the oven to 100 °C.

Put the eggs, yolks and 125 grams of sugar in a mixing bowl and beat until frothy.

Bring the milk to the boil with 100 grams of granulated sugar and the vanilla and pour over the beaten eggs, stirring constantly. Pass through a sieve.

Carefully pour the mixture over the caramel into the ramekins.

Place the roasting tray with the ramekins in the pre-heated oven and cook for 1 hour until the cream has set nicely.

Remove the ramekins from the roasting tray and place in the refrigerator to cool.

Loosen the edges with a sharp knife, place the ramekin upside down on a plate. Tap the bottom of the plate briefly so that the cream comes loose and the sauce flows over the crème.

AGA

Make the caramel on the simmering plate.
Place the roasting pan at the top of the
slow cooking oven.

TIP

Dry sugar burns easily so always put some cold water
into the pan before adding sugar.
Pour the crème over a tablespoon that you hold in the
ramekins to shield the caramel layer and prevent the
crème and caramel from mixing.
The crème will solidify when cooled in the refrigerator.

TO SERVE 4

FOR THE FILLING:
3 apples, peeled and diced
2 pears, peeled and diced
40 g butter
60 g cane sugar
150 g gingerbread, in 0.5 cm cubes
40 g butter
2 dl cream 40%

FOR THE CRUMBLE:
80 g gingerbread
80 g speculaas (cinnamon biscuits)
60 g flour
10 g vanilla sugar
100 g cold butter, cut into small lumps

Gingerbread crumble with apple and pear

FILLING
Fry the diced apple and pear in the butter with the cane sugar until crispy. Place in an oven dish.

Briefly fry the gingerbread in the butter and arrange on top of the apple and pear.

Pour the cream over it.

CRUMBLE
Pre-heat the oven to 200 °C.

Mix the gingerbread, speculaas, flour and vanilla sugar into crumbs.

Add the pieces of cold butter and mix into to a sandy crumble.

Spread the crumble across the oven dish.

Bake for 10 minutes in the pre-heated oven.

AGA

Fry the fruit and gingerbread on the boiling plate. Place the oven dish on the bottom of the roasting oven.

TO SERVE 4

- 12 tablespoons gin
- 1 cinnamon stick + 4 extra sticks to garnish
- butter for greasing the ramekins
- 200 g strawberries, cleaned and cut
- 200 g raspberries
- 200 g red berries, without sprigs
- 1 egg
- 30 g icing sugar
- 250 g of quark
- 20 leaves of mint

Red fruit with quark

Pre-heat the oven to 200 °C.

Boil the gin for about 1 minutes with the cinnamon stick.

Butter an oven dish and distribute the red fruit on it. Drizzle with the gin and cover with aluminium foil or baking paper.

Bake for 6 minutes in the pre-heated oven.

Separate the egg and beat the egg white until stiff.

Mix the egg yolk with the icing sugar and the quark and fold the egg white into this mixture.

Finish the baked red fruit with a spoonful of the quark mixture, five mint leaves and a cinnamon stick.

AGA

Place the little oven dishes at the top of the roasting oven.

TIP

Replace the mint with basil.

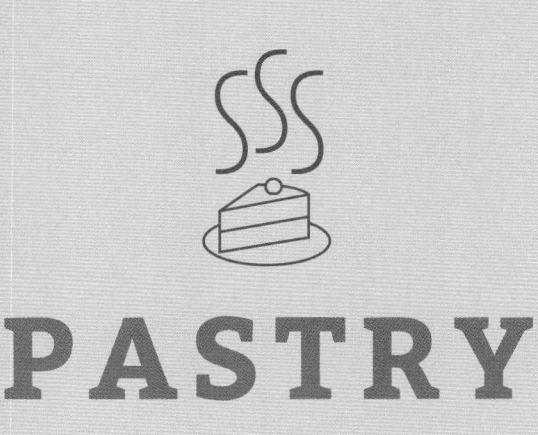

PASTRY

Pastry: classics with a twist

Baking is both simple and an art in itself, which I have really come to enjoy over the years. It has a relaxing effect and fills my kitchen with the most delicious smells. I prefer tasty traditional cakes and pies such as a quatre-quarts or an apple pie as well as a tartine russe, misérable or 'billygoat hoofs'. And never be afraid to give an original twist to shape or finish here and there. Let yourself be inspired!

FOR 1 APPLE STRUDEL

FOR THE FRANGIPANE:
500 g almond flour
150 g flour
8 grams vanilla sugar
500 g butter, at room temperature
9 eggs

FOR THE APPLE STRUDEL:
2 tablespoons raisins
2 apples, peeled and cut into small pieces
dash of brown rum
1 square piece of puff pastry, cut in half
1 egg yolk, beaten
icing sugar

Apple strudel

FRANGIPANE

Mix the almond flour with the flour and vanilla sugar.

Smooth the butter in a food processor with a beater.

Add the almond flour mixture and eggs alternately to the butter and beat the batter vigorously.

APPLE STRUDEL

Pre-heat the oven to 200 °C.

Soak the raisins and the apple pieces in the rum.

Place a sheet of baking paper or a baking mat on a baking tray.

Arrange both pieces of puff pastry next to each other on this.

Prick the left piece with a fork and spread with the frangipane batter. Stay 1 centimetre from the edge.

Arrange the drained raisins and apple pieces on the batter.

Cut the second sheet of puff pastry cross-wise every centimetre with the tip of a knife, keeping 1 centimetre from the edge.

Place the cut sheet of puff pastry on top of the filling and press the sides firmly with your fingers.

Brush with the beaten egg yolk.

Bake for 25 minutes in the pre-heated oven.

Sprinkle with the icing sugar.

AGA

Place the baking tray on the bottom of the roasting oven.

FOR A Ø 22 CM SPRINGFORM DISH

8 small stewed pears, peeled and diced
0.5 dl Marsala
130 g butter, at room temperature
4 eggs
150 g sugar
1 teaspoon almond extract
200 g self-raising flour
50 g ground almonds
30 g cane sugar
50 g flaked almonds
icing sugar

Almond cake with pear

Pre-heat the oven to 180 °C.

Marinate the diced pear in the marsala for 30 minutes.

Beat the butter, eggs, sugar, almond extract, self-raising flour and ground almonds briefly and vigorously in a food processor with a beater.

Place a sheet of baking paper in the springform, spoon in the dough and smooth it out.

Spread the marinated pear across the dough and sprinkle with the cane sugar.

Bake for 45 minutes in the pre-heated oven.

Let the cake cool, remove from the tin, and sprinkle with the almonds and icing sugar.

AGA

Place the cake in the middle of the baking oven.

FOR 60 AMARETTI

250 g self-raising flour, sifted
1.5 tablespoons gingerbread spices
pinch of salt
200 g apple syrup
100 g cold butter, cut into small blocks
2 tablespoons milk

Amaretti

Mix all ingredients except the milk in a food processor with a K beater.

Add the milk and knead until you can form a ball of the dough.

Wrap the dough in cling film and leave for least 30 minutes in the refrigerator.

Pre-heat the oven to 170 °C.

Place a sheet of baking paper or a baking mat on a baking tray.

Roll small 2 cm balls from the dough, place them on the baking tray and flatten them slightly.

Bake for 12 to 14 minutes in the pre-heated oven.

Leave on a wire rack to cool.

AGA

Place the baking tray on the bottom of the baking oven.

FOR A Ø 24 CM TART TIN

FOR THE APPLESAUCE:
4 apples, peeled and cut into equal pieces
60 g sugar
10 g vanilla sugar
20 g butter

FOR THE TART:
100 g raisins
50 g brown rum
1 sheet of puff pastry
150 g sugar
150 g butter, at room temperature
3 eggs
150 g self-raising flour

Applesauce tart

APPLE SAUCE
Stew the apples with the sugar, vanilla sugar and butter under a lid into an apple sauce and stir occasionally.

CAKE
Pre-heat the oven to 180 °C.

Soak the raisins in the brown rum.

Place the puff pastry with the baking paper in the tart tin and prick with a fork.

Spread the apple sauce across the base.

Beat the sugar with the butter into a light yellow mass in a food processor with a beater.

Leave the food processor running and add the eggs one by one.

Sift the self-raising flour over the mixture and beat to a dough.

Mix the drained raisins into the dough.

Pour the mixture on top of the apple sauce and smooth.

Bake for 30 minutes in the pre-heated oven.

AGA

Make the apple sauce on the simmering plate.
Place the pie dish in the middle of the baking oven.

FOR A 25 x 38 20 CM BISCUIT TRAY
245 g sugar
5 eggs
contents of 1 vanilla pod
1 teaspoon red food colouring
190 g flour
95 g cornflour
5 g baking powder
icing sugar

Biscuit rose

Pre-heat the oven to 180 °C.

Beat the sugar, eggs and the vanilla until fluffy in a food processor with a beater.

Add the red colouring and beat further.

Sift the flour, cornflour and baking powder and fold into the batter.

Place a sheet of baking paper on the bottom of a biscuit tray, spoon the dough on top and smooth with a palette knife.

Bake for 15 minutes in the pre-heated oven.

Lower the temperature to 120 °C.

Remove the biscuit from the tray and cut into elongated individual biscuits.

Return the biscuits to the tray with baking paper and sprinkle with icing sugar.
Bake in the pre-heated oven for 15 minutes until crispy.

Leave on a wire rack to cool.

AGA

Place the biscuit tray in the middle of the baking oven. Place the biscuit tin with the cut biscuits in the simmering oven.

TIP

Serve the biscuits with a glass of champagne. Dunking is allowed.

FOR A Ø 20 CM TART TIN

FOR THE BUTTER DOUGH:
100 g butter, at room temperature
100 g dark brown sugar
1 egg + 1 extra yolk
250 g flour, sifted
pinch of salt
10 g ground almonds

FOR THE APPLE PIE:
40 g butter
60 g sugar
2 egg yolks
10 g cornflour
5 Jonagold apples, peeled, in equal cubes and drizzled with the juice of ½ lemon

2 tablespoons apricot jam
dash of water
2 tablespoons icing sugar

Apple pie

BUTTER DOUGH

Put the butter in a bowl and mix in the sugar with one hand.

Add the egg and egg yolk and mix well.

Add the flour and salt and knead into a firm dough. Add a little extra flour if the dough sticks.

Make a ball, roll into a sausage and wrap in cling film. Leave to cool for at least 30 minutes in the refrigerator.

Knead the dough once again and roll out slightly larger than the pie dish on a floured work surface.

Butter the pie dish, sprinkle with the ground almonds and place the dough in the pie dish.

APPLE PIE

Pre-heat the oven to 175 °C.

Melt the butter with the sugar over a very low heat.

Add the egg yolks and beat until frothy.

Fold the cornflour gently into the mixture.

Mix the pieces of apple into the batter.

Pour the batter onto the butter dough in the pie dish.

Bake the pie for 15 minutes in the pre-heated oven.

Reduce the temperature to 160 °C and bake for another 15 minutes.

Boil the apricot jam briefly with a splash of water, strain and brush over the pie.

Garnish with the icing sugar.

AGA

Place the pie dish in the middle of the baking oven.
Then move the pie dish to the bottom of the baking oven.
Boil the jam on the boiling plate.

FOR AN 18 x 18 CM SQUARE SPRINGFORM

- 2 apples, peeled and cut into 0.5 cm cubes
- 25 g butter
- 3 tablespoons honey
- 3 eggs
- 100 g fine caster sugar
- 180 g butter, at room temperature
- 100 g ground almonds
- 180 g self-raising flour, sifted
- pinch of salt
- 180 g blueberries

Blueberry cake

Pre-heat the oven to 175 °C.

Caramelise the apple cubes in the butter and honey in a non-stick pan. Reserve.

Beat the eggs and the sugar into a white mass in a food processor with a beater. Add the soft butter and continue beating.

Fold the ground almonds, self-raising flour and salt into the mixture.

Fold the caramelized apple into the dough.

Spoon the dough into a buttered and floured springform.

Divide the blueberries over the dough and press them lightly.

Bake for 55 minutes in the pre-heated oven.

AGA

Caramelize the apple on the boiling plate.
Place the springform on the bottom of the baking oven.

FOR 15 BROWNIES

250 g chocolate, grated
220 g butter
380 g sugar
6 eggs
150 g self-raising flour
70 g flaked almonds
icing sugar for finishing

Brownies

Pre-heat the oven to 170 °C.

Melt the chocolate with the butter on a low heat and allow to cool briefly.

Mix the sugar, eggs and the self-raising flour in a food processor with a beater.

Add the melted chocolate and mix.

Add the flaked almonds and mix again.

Place a sheet of baking paper in a rectangular baking tin and spoon the dough 2 cm thick onto it.

Bake for 25 minutes in the pre-heated oven.

Leave on a wire rack to cool.

Cut into squares. Serve sprinkled with icing sugar.

AGA

Melt the chocolate with the butter on the simmering plate.
Place the baking tin on the bottom of the baking oven.

TIP

Brownies are crispy on top and creamy soft on the inside.

FOR 10 STICKS

- 8 egg whites
- pinch of salt
- 200 g sugar
- 180 g ground almonds
- 180 g icing sugar
- 40 g flour
- 150 g flaked almonds
- 10 tablespoons apricot jam
- 250 g dark chocolate, broken into pieces

Chocolate-tipped meringue sticks (billygoat hoofs)

Pre-heat the oven to 190 °C.

Beat the egg whites with the salt and half of the sugar until fluffy in a food processor with a beater. Add the remaining sugar and beat into a stiff mass. Reserve.

Mix the ground almonds, icing sugar and flour and fold in the beaten egg whites.

Place into a piping bag with a serrated nozzle.

Place a sheet of baking paper or a baking mat on a baking tray.

Spray even strips about 8 centimetres in length and make sure there is sufficient space between them. Sprinkle with the flaked almonds.

Bake for 8 minutes in the pre-heated oven.

Leave to cool.

Cover the smooth side of the meringues with jam and stick two meringues together.

Melt 150 grams of chocolate to 40 °C and stir in the rest of the chocolate. Cool to 32 ° C and dip the ends of the billygoat's hoofs in the chocolate. Leave to stiffen.

AGA

Place the baking tray in the middle of the baking oven.

TIP

Always beat egg whites in a degreased bowl. Degrease the bowl with vinegar, vodka or gin.

FOR 60 BISCUITS

200 g dark chocolate, grated
50 g butter
120 g sugar
8 g vanilla sugar
3 eggs
180 g self-raising flour
30 g cocoa powder
icing sugar

Cocoa biscuits

Melt the chocolate with the butter on a low heat and leave to cool briefly.

Beat the melted chocolate, sugar, vanilla sugar and eggs to a froth in a food processor with a beater.

Add the self-raising flour and cocoa powder and mix to a dough with a K-beater.

Make a ball of the dough and wrap in cling film. Leave for 15 minutes in the refrigerator.

Pre-heat the oven to 160 °C.

Place a sheet of baking paper or a baking mat on a baking tray.

Roll 2.5 cm balls with wet hands, place on the baking tray and flatten. slightly.

Bake for 20 minutes in the pre-heated oven.

Dust with icing sugar.

AGA

Melt the chocolate with the butter on the simmering plate.
Place the baking tray on the bottom of the baking oven and cover with a sheet of baking paper.

FOR A Ø 24 CM CAKE MOULD

275 g brown sugar
7 eggs
250 g butter, at room temperature
90 g pure cocoa powder
150 g hazelnut flour
extra butter to grease the tart tin pan
150 g mixed nuts and dried fruit
120 g fine granulated sugar
water
icing sugar

Chocolate cake with hazelnut

Pre-heat the oven to 160 °C.

Beat the brown sugar and eggs to a froth in a food processor with a beater.

Stir the butter and cocoa powder into a homogeneous mass and add. Add the hazelnut flour and beat until smooth.

Place the batter into a buttered silicone cake mould.

Bake for 40 minutes in the pre-heated oven.

Leave in the cake mould on a wire rack to cool. Remove from the mould.

Divide the mixed nuts and dried fruit over the bottom of the silicone cake pan.

Melt the sugar with a splash of water in a pan without stirring until the caramel is golden brown. Deglaze with a splash of water and beat the caramel until smooth.

Pour the caramel over the nuts in the silicone cake mould and leave to cool.

Finish the cake with the caramelized nuts and the icing sugar.

AGA

Place the baking mould on the bottom of the baking oven and cover for the first 20 minutes with a sheet of baking paper.
Make the caramel on the boiling plate.

FOR TEN BARS

120 g cream

120 g chocolate, broken into lumps

1 sheet of puff pastry

2 egg yolks, beaten

50 g rough-grated almonds

icing sugar

Chocolate bars

Pre-heat the oven to 180 °C.

Heat the cream to 80 °C and melt the chocolate into it. Stir until smooth and place in a piping bag.

Place a sheet of baking paper or a baking mat on a baking tray.

Cut the puff pastry into 7.5-centimetre slices.

Pipe a line of chocolate on the right side of each strip of puff pastry. Brush the left side with egg yolk, roll up and arrange on the baking tray.

Brush with egg yolk and sprinkle with the grated almonds.

Bake for 20 minutes in the pre-heated oven.

Decorate with the icing sugar.

AGA

Place the baking tray in the middle of the baking oven.

FOR A Ø 25 CM TURBAN CAKE MOULD

250 g butter, at room temperature
250 g sugar
8 g vanilla sugar
4 eggs
250 ground almonds
75 g flour

Frangipane cake

Pre-heat the oven to 175 °C.

Beat the butter, the sugar and vanilla sugar in a food processor with a beater.

Leave the food processor running and add the eggs one by one.

Add the ground almonds and the flour and mix with a K-beater.

Place the mixture into a buttered turban cake mould.

Bake for 30 minutes in the pre-heated oven.

Lower the temperature to 160 °C. Place a sheet of baking paper on top of the cake and bake for a further 10 minutes.

Leave to cool and remove from the mould.

AGA

Place the cake on the bottom of the baking oven. After 30 minutes, slide a cold plate just above the cake and leave to it bake for further 10 minutes.

FOR A Ø 25 CM TURBAN CAKE MOULD

- 250 g butter, at room temperature
- 250 g sugar
- contents of 1 vanilla pod
- 5 eggs
- juice and zest of ½ lemon
- 200 g flour
- 50 g cornflour
- 5 g baking powder
- butter for greasing the turban cake mould
- 2 tablespoons apricot jam
- 2 tablespoons water
- 1 cinnamon stick
- 1 star anise
- 4 juniper berries
- pulp of ½ lemon and strips of the peel

Lemon sand cake

Pre-heat the oven to 180 °C.

Beat the butter, the sugar and the vanilla in a food processor with a beater.

Leave the food processor running and add the eggs one by one.

Add zest and juice of 1/2 lemon.

Mix the flour, cornflour and baking powder into the batter with a K-beater.

Fill a buttered turban cake mould 2/3 full with the mixture.

Bake for 30 to 35 minutes in the pre-heated oven.

Place a sheet of baking paper on top of the cake and bake for a further 15 minutes.

Heat the jam and water over a low heat and add the cinnamon stick, star anise, juniper berries and slices of lemon peel. Allow to draw for a while.

Remove the cake from the mould and leave on a wire rack to cool.

Pour the jelly over the cake and decorate with the spices, lemon pulp and lemon zest.

AGA

Place the cake in the middle of the baking oven.
Heat the jam on the simmering plate.

FOR A Ø 24 CM CAKE MOULD

- 200 g raisins
- Amaretto
- 250 g butter, at room temperature
- 250 g sugar
- 4 eggs
- 200 g flour
- 5 g baking powder
- 100 g peeled almonds, chopped + extra for decoration
- 2 tablespoons apricot jam
- 2 tablespoons water

Dundee Cake

Put the raisins in the Amaretto and leave to soak for 1 hour. Drain.

Pre-heat the oven to 180 °C.

Beat the butter and the sugar in a food processor with a beater.

Leave the food processor running and add the eggs one by one.

Add the flour and baking powder and mix with a K-beater.

Mix the raisins and almonds into the batter.

Bake for 40 minutes in the pre-heated oven.

Remove from the mould and leave to cool.

Heat the jam and water on a low heat and brush the cake with it.

Decorate with some peeled almonds.

AGA

Place the cake in the middle of the baking oven. Heat the jam on the simmering plate.

TIP

Dundee cake is a traditional Scottish fruitcake developed in Dundee in the late 17th century. Since the Scottish Queen Mary was not a fan of the candied cherries in the cake, they were replaced with almonds. It is said that Queen Elisabeth II also likes a piece with her tea.

FOR A Ø 18 CM SPRINGFORM

- 120 g butter, at room temperature
- 100 g brown sugar
- 1 egg
- 100 g dark chocolate, finely chopped
- 180 g wheat flour, sifted
- 90 g ground almonds
- 90 g ground hazelnuts
- 2 teaspoons baking powder
- 1 tablespoon chocolate chips

Chocolate cookie with hazelnut

Pre-heat the oven to 175 °C.

Mix the butter with the dark sugar in a food processor with a K beater. Add the egg, chocolate, wheat flour, ground almonds, ground hazelnuts and baking powder.

Place a sheet of baking paper in a springform and spoon in the dough. Smooth.

Bake for 20 to 25 minutes in the pre-heated oven.

Leave to cool in the mould.

Remove the cake from the mould and finish with the chocolate chips.

AGA

Place the cake on the bottom of the baking oven.

TIP

While the outside of the cake should be crispy, the inside can still be 'raw'.

FOR FORTY BISCUITS

100 g sugar
200 g butter, at room temperature
6 tablespoons honey
content of 1 vanilla pod
350 g flour
pinch of salt
extra sugar

Honey biscuits

Beat the sugar, butter, honey and vanilla in a food processor with a K beater.

Leave the food processor running and gradually add the flour and salt.

Place the dough on a sheet of cling film and roll into a sausage about 2 centimetres in diameter.

Leave to stiffen in the refrigerator.

Pre-heat the oven to 175 °C.

Place a sheet of baking paper or a baking mat on a baking tray.

Sprinkle some more sugar on a plate and roll the dough in it.

Cut 1-centimetre-thick biscuits and arrange them on the baking tray.

Bake for 15 minutes in the pre-heated oven. Leave on a wire rack to cool.

AGA

Place the baking tray in the middle of the baking oven.

FOR A Ø 26 CM PIE MOULD
FOR THE SEMOLINA
PUDDING:
5 dl whole milk
30 g sugar
8 g vanilla sugar
70 g semolina
1 egg yolk
1 egg white

FOR THE CHERRY FILLING:
240 g Amarena cherries
(sour cherries in sugar syrup
50 g sugar

20 g cornflour
2 tablespoons cold water

FOR THE FLAN:
2 sheets of puff pastry
butter and flour
1 egg yolk, beaten

Cherry flan

SEMOLINA PUDDING
Bring the milk to the boil with the sugar and the vanilla sugar. Add the semolina, stirring all the time, and bring back to the boil. Cover, remove from heat and leave for 15 minutes.

Once lukewarm, mix the egg yolk into the pudding.

Beat the egg white until stiff and fold into the pudding.

Put the pudding into a piping bag and leave to rest in the refrigerator.

CHERRY FILLING
Drain the cherries and collect the liquid.

Add water to the cherry juice to give 1.25 dl.

Bring the cherry juice to the boil and melt the sugar into it.

Mix the cornflour with the water and add while stirring. Leave to cook for 1 minute. Add the cherries, stir and leave to cool in the refrigerator.

FLAN
Pre-heat the oven to 200 °C.

Place a sheet of puff pastry in a buttered and floured pie mould. Push the sides in firmly and leave the dough hanging over the edge. Brush the edges with beaten egg yolk.

Prick the bottom with a fork.

Pipe a layer of semolina pudding onto the bottom.

Spread the cherry filling across the semolina pudding.

Work the second sheet of puff pastry with a flan press-out grid or roller to give an open grid pattern.

Place the grid on the flan.

Press the edges equally with the fingers. Roll off the excess dough.

Brush the grid with beaten egg yolk.

Bake for 20 minutes in the pre-heated oven.

AGA

Make the semolina pudding on the simmering plate.
Leave the semolina pudding to rest in the
slow cooking oven.
Boil the cherry juice on the boiling plate.
Place the flan mould on the bottom of the roasting oven.

TIP

The semolina pudding can be made a day in advance.
A flan press-out cutter or a flan roller is available in the
cookery shop.
A grid shape in puff pastry is also available in the frozen
foods section.

FOR 24 BISCUITS
250 g butter
115 g sugar
30 g icing sugar
0.5 dl milk

330 g flour
3 g salt
200 g sugar for the topping
2 teaspoons cinnamon

Cinnamon sprites

Pre-heat the oven to 170 °C.

Place a sheet of baking paper or a baking mat on a baking tray.

Beat the butter, sugar and icing sugar in a food processor with a beater.

Add the milk and continue beating.

Leave the food processor running and gradually add the flour and salt.

Place in a piping bag with a serrated nozzle and pipe the sprites.

Bake for 15 minutes in the pre-heated oven.

Place on a wire rack to cool.

Mix the sugar with the cinnamon powder and sprinkle over the sprites.

AGA

Place the baking tray on the bottom of the baking oven.

Christmas cake

FOR A Ø 25 CM TURBAN CAKE MOULD

- 175 g butter, at room temperature
- 240 g light brown caster sugar
- 8 g vanilla sugar
- 3 eggs
- ½ teaspoon vanilla extract
- 2 teaspoons almond extract
- 200 g self-raising flour, sifted
- 170 g Greek yoghurt
- 1 teaspoon mixed spices
- 50 g roasted flaked almonds
- 100 g fresh cranberries
- 100 g marzipan, cut into 0.5 cm cubes
- 2 tablespoons icing sugar

Pre-heat the oven to 175 °C.

Beat the butter, brown caster sugar and vanilla sugar in a food processor with a beater.

Leave the food processor running and add the eggs one by one.

Add the vanilla extract, the almond extract, the self-raising flour, the yoghurt and the mixed spices and mix to a smooth dough with the K-Beater.

Mix the flaked almonds and cranberries into the dough.

Roll the cubes of marzipan in the icing sugar and mix into the dough

Pour the batter into a buttered and floured cake mould and smooth with a palette knife.

Bake for 45 minutes in the pre-heated oven.

Remove the cake from the mould and leave on a wire rack to cool.

Sprinkle with icing sugar for a snowy effect

AGA

Place the cake mould on the bottom of the baking oven.

FOR 20 ALMOND SNAPS

250 g candy sugar

75 g butter, at room temperature

60 g flaked almonds

125 g flour

50 g of water

Almond snaps ('chatterboxes')

Pre-heat the oven to 200 °C.

Mix all the ingredients in a food processor with a K-beater to a smooth dough.

Place the dough on a sheet of cling film, roll up to a sausage 4 centimetres and place in the refrigerator for 3 hours.

Place a sheet of baking paper or a baking mat on a baking tray.

Cut the dough roll into thin slices and place them far enough apart on the baking tray.

Bake for 8 to 10 minutes in the pre-heated oven.

Immediately remove the biscuits from the baking tray with a palette knife and allow to cool and become crispy on a wire rack.

Repeat until the dough is all used up.

AGA

Place the baking tray on the bottom of the roasting oven.

TIP

You can also roll balls from the dough and press them flat on the baking tray.

FOR A 9 x 26 CM CAKE MOULD

200 g butter, at room temperature
200 g sugar
4 eggs
100 g flour
100 g cornflour
125 g grated coconut
5 g baking powder
2 tablespoons apricot jam
2 tablespoons water

extra grated coconut to decorate

Coconut bar

Pre-heat the oven to 180 °C.

Beat the butter and the sugar in the food processor with a beater.

Leave the food processor running and add the eggs one by one.

Add the flour, cornflour, ground coconut and baking powder and beat to a creamy dough.

Place the mixture into a buttered cake mould.

Bake for 35 minutes in the pre-heated oven.

Leave to cool.

Heat the jam with the water and stir into a jelly.

Spread the top and sides of the cake with the jelly and sprinkle with grated coconut.

AGA

Place the cake mould in the middle of the baking oven. Heat the jam on the simmering plate.

FOR A Ø 20 CM SPRINGFORM

FOR THE BISCUIT:
5 egg whites
100 g icing sugar
250 g ground almonds
120 g caster sugar
40 g self-raising flour, sifted
1 drop of almond extract

FOR THE TOPPING
2 egg yolks
45 g icing sugar
250 g mascarpone
2 egg whites
80 g cream 40%

FOR THE DECORATION:
4 tablespoons chocolate chips
2 fresh figs, in wedges
12 raspberries
100 g blueberries
a few leaves of mint
some basil flowers

Misérable

BISCUIT

Pre-heat the oven to 180 °C.

Beat the egg whites stiff in a food processor with a beater and add the icing sugar at the end.

Mix together the ground almonds, caster sugar and self-raising flour and carefully fold the mixture with the almond extract into the beaten egg whites.

Place a sheet of baking paper in the springform and spoon in the mixture. Smooth flat with a palette knife.

Bake for 25 minutes in the pre-heated oven.

Reduce the temperature to 120 ° C and bake for another 8 minutes to dry.

Place on a wire rack to cool.

TOPPING

Stir the egg yolks and icing sugar into the mascarpone.

Beat the egg whites until stiff.

Whip the cream until stiff.

Fold first the cream and then the egg whites carefully into the mascarpone mixture.

Brush the top and sides of the biscuit with a thick layer of mascarpone mixture.

Cover the side of the biscuit with the chocolate chips, using a palette knife.

Arrange the fruit on the tart and decorate with the mint leaves and basil flowers.

AGA

Place the springform in the middle of the baking oven.
Transfer the springform to the slow cooking oven.

FOR A Ø 25 CM TURBAN CAKE MOULD

FOR THE CAKE:
4 eggs
200 g granulated sugar, fine
1 sachet vanilla sugar
200 g self-raising flour
pinch of salt
200 g butter, at room temperature
1 tablespoon vanilla essence

FOR THE SALTED CARAMEL:
50 g butter
175 g brown sugar
½ teaspoon salt
1 teaspoon vanilla essence
150 g cream

FOR THE DECORATION:
4 tablespoons Brazil nuts

Nut cake with salted caramel

CAKE

Pre-heat the oven to 175 °C.

Beat the eggs, sugar and vanilla sugar till fluffy in a food processor with a beater.

Add the self-raising flour, salt, butter and vanilla essence, and beat to a smooth dough.

Place the dough into a buttered silicone turban mould and place on a baking tray.

Bake for 40 minutes in the pre-heated oven.

Remove the cake from the mould and leave on a wire rack to cool.

CARAMEL

Melt the butter and the sugar over a low heat.

Add the salt, vanilla essence and cream and allow to thicken over a low heat.

Pour the caramel over the cake and finish with the Brazil nuts.

AGA

Place the baking tray on the bottom of the baking oven. Melt the butter and the sugar on the simmering plate.

FOR 25 ROCKS

100 g egg whites, beaten

200 g fine granulated sugar

180 g ground coconut

10 g flour

Coconut rocks

Place a sheet of baking paper or a baking mat on a baking tray.

Beat the egg white and sugar over a low heat to 37 °C.

Remove from heat and beat until the mass has cooled completely.

Fold in the ground coconut and the flour into a homogeneous mixture.

Put the mixture into a piping bag with a serrated mouth and pipe solid dollops onto the baking tray.

Bake in the pre-heated oven for 8 minutes until golden brown and crispy on the outside and soft on the inside.

AGA

Beat the egg white and sugar on the simmering plate. Place the baking tray as high as possible in the baking oven.

TIP

You can keep the coconut rocks in a biscuit tin for a few weeks.
Sugar melts at 37 °C, which makes for a much more airy mixture. Just make sure that the temperature does not get higher.

FOR 20 BISCUITS

380 g flour
1.5 tablespoons ground ginger
1 teaspoon cinnamon spices
1 teaspoon baking soda
100 g candy sugar
150 g Liège syrup
150 g butter, at room temperature
pinch of salt
1 egg yolk

Gingerbread

Pre-heat the oven to 180 °C.

Place a sheet of baking paper or a baking mat on a baking tray.

Mix all the ingredients in a food processor with a K-beater to a dough and knead for 1 minute.

Wrap the dough in cling film and leave for an hour in the refrigerator.

Place the mixture onto a sheet of baking paper. Place a second sheet of baking paper on top and roll out the dough to 4 millimetres thick.

Cut out biscuit shapes from the dough with a biscuit cutter and arrange on the baking tray.

Bake for 8 to 10 minutes in the pre-heated oven.

Place on a wire rack to cool.

AGA

Place the baking tray in the middle of the baking oven.

FOR A Ø 24 CM SPRINGFORM

175 g butter, at room temperature
150 g brown sugar
3 eggs
50 g almonds, roughly chopped
150 g self-raising flour, sifted
1 teaspoon vanilla pudding powder
50 g almond flour
pinch of salt
2 conference pears, peeled and diced
40 g flaked almonds
30 g icing sugar

Pear tart with almonds

Pre-heat the oven to 175 °C.

Cream the butter and the sugar together in a food processor with a beater.

Leave the food processor running and add the eggs one by one.

Add the chopped almonds, self-raising flour, vanilla pudding powder, almond flour and salt and mix with the K-beater.

Mix in the diced pears.

Place a sheet of baking paper in a springform and spoon in the mixture. Sprinkle with the flaked almonds and icing sugar.

Bake for 35 to 40 minutes in the pre-heated oven.

Leave to cool and remove from the mould.

AGA

Place the springform on the bottom of the baking oven.

FOR A 9 x 26 CM CAKE MOULD

250 g butter, at room temperature
250 g sugar
4 eggs
250 g self-raising flour

Quatre-quarts cake

Pre-heat the oven to 175 °C.

Cream the butter and the sugar till light and airy in a food processor with a beater.

Leave the food processor running and add the eggs one by one.

Spoon in the sifted flour, one half at a time, and mix well.

Place the mixture into a buttered baking mould.

Bake for 35 to 40 minutes in the pre-heated oven.

Remove from the mould and leave on a wire rack to cool.

AGA

Place the baking mould on the bottom of the baking oven.

FOR A 9 x 26 CM CAKE MOULD
Mixture for 1 quatre-quarts cake (p. xx)
30 g calvados
25 g flaked almonds
1 apple, finely sliced
15 g fine caster sugar
2 tablespoons apricot jam
2 tablespoons water

Quatre-quarts apple cake

Pre-heat the oven to 175 °C.

Mix the calvados into the basic dough.

Spread the flaked almonds across the base of a buttered baking mould.

Pour half of the mixture into the baking tin and arrange a layer of apple slices on top. Cover with the rest of the mixture.

Arrange a layer of apple slices on top of the mixture and sprinkle with the caster sugar.

Bake for 35 to 40 minutes in the pre-heated oven.

Remove from the mould and leave on a wire rack to cool.

Heat the jam with the water and brush the cake with it.

AGA

Place the baking tin on the bottom of the baking oven. Heat the jam on the simmering plate.

FOR A 9 x 26 CM CAKE MOULD
200 g butter, at room temperature
120 g sugar
4 egg yolks
200 g self-raising flour
100 g gingerbread, finely cut
1 apple, peeled and diced finely
4 egg whites

Quatre-quarts gingerbread-apple cake

Pre-heat the oven to 175 °C.

Cream the butter and the sugar until light and airy in a food processor with a beater.

Leave the food processor running and add the yolks one by one.

Spoon in the sifted flour, one half at a time, and mix well.

Mix in gingerbread and apple.

Beat the egg whites and fold into the mixture.

Place the mixture into a buttered baking mould.

Bake for 35 to 40 minutes in the pre-heated oven.

Remove from the mould and leave on a wire rack to cool.

AGA

Place the baking mould on the bottom of the baking oven.

TIP

Chop the apple very fine so that it doesn't sink to the bottom of the cake during baking.

Quatre-quarts apple cake

Quatre-quarts gingerbread-apple cake

Quatre-quarts cake

FOR A Ø 24 CM TART MOULD
1 sheet of puff pastry
5 dl whole milk
5 dl coconut milk
content of 1 vanilla pod
180 g sugar
130 g dessert rice
50 g vanilla pudding powder

dash of milk
2 egg yolks
juice of 3 limes
zest of ½ lime
2 egg whites
icing sugar
zest of 1 lime

Rice tart with coconut

Place the sheet of puff pastry with baking paper in a cake tin and press the edges down well with your fingers. Prick the bottom with a fork and roll off the edges.

Boil the milk, coconut milk, vanilla, sugar and dessert rice for 25 minutes, stirring frequently.

Pre-heat the oven to 175 °C.

Remove the rice from the heat, stir the vanilla pudding powder into the milk and mix into the cooked rice.

Add the egg yolks and stir well.

Mix the lime juice and lime zest into the rice.

Beat the egg white until stiff and fold into the rice pudding.

Pour the rice pudding into the tart mould.

Bake for 45 minutes in the pre-heated oven.

Leave to cool and finish with icing sugar and lime zest.

AGA

Bring the milk, coconut milk, vanilla, sugar and dessert rice to the boil on the simmering plate and place in the slow cooking oven, under a lid, for 90 minutes. You don't need to stir.
Place the tart mould on the bottom of the baking oven.

FOR A Ø 20 CM TART MOULD

1 litre of whole milk	3 eggs
65 g sugar	75 g ground almonds
8 threads of saffron	½ teaspoon vanilla extract
¼ teaspoon salt	pinch of cinnamon
220 g dessert rice	icing sugar

Rice tart express

Pre-heat the oven to 180 °C.

Boil the milk, sugar, saffron, salt and dessert rice for 25 minutes, stirring frequently.

Mix the eggs, ground almonds, vanilla extract and cinnamon.

Remove the rice from the heat and mix the egg mixture into the cooked rice.

Place the mixture into a buttered tart mould.

Bake for 25 minutes in the pre-heated oven.

Place in the mould on a wire rack to cool.

Sprinkle with icing sugar.

AGA

Bring the milk, sugar, saffron and salt and dessert rice to the boil on the simmering plate and place in the slow cooking oven, under a lid, for 45 minutes. You don't need to stir.
Place the tart mould in the middle of the baking oven.

FOR A Ø 24 CM ROUND OVEN DISH

- 255 g whole milk
- 255 g cream
- 25 g sugar
- 1 vanilla pod, cut lengthwise
- 4 egg yolks, beaten
- 400 g biscuit bread (milk bread), without crusts and broken into pieces

Fast bread pudding

Pre-heat the oven to 200 °C.

Bring the milk, cream and sugar to the boil and add the vanilla pod.

Add the egg yolks and beat over a low heat.

Divide the biscuit bread over a buttered oven dish and cover with the mixture. Lay the vanilla pod on top and cover with aluminium foil.

Leave for 20 minutes.

Remove the foil and bake for 20 minutes in the pre-heated oven.

AGA

Boil on the simmering plate.
Place the oven dish on the bottom of the roasting oven.

FOR A Ø 26 CM SPRINGFORM

FOR THE ORANGE TART:
200 g salted butter
300 + 80 g sugar
zest and juice of 4 oranges
zest and juice of 1 lemon
245 g almond flour
5 eggs
135 self-raising flour
pinch of salt

FOR THE LIQUEUR:
400 g cream 40%
150 g candy sugar
10 g orange zest
80 g orange juice (= 2 oranges)
100 g white chocolate, broken into pieces
1 egg
300 g whisky

Orange tart with liqueur

ORANGE TART

Pre-heat the oven to 180 °C.

Place a sheet of baking paper on the bottom of the springform and butter the bottom and the edges.

Mix the butter, 300 grams of sugar, the zest of the oranges and lemon and half of the almond flour in the food processor with a beater on low speed.

Leave the food processor running and add the eggs one by one.

Add the flour, salt and the rest of the almond flour and mix well.

Place the mixture into the springform and smooth with a palette knife.

Bake for 45 minutes in the pre-heated oven.

Place on a wire rack to cool.

Bring the orange and lemon juice and 80 grams of sugar to the boil and reduce to a syrup.

Pour the syrup over the cake.

LIQUEUR

Mix all ingredients except the whisky in a blender for 10 seconds.

Pour into a saucepan and heat to 70 °C while stirring.

Add the whisky and mix.

Let cool and drizzle onto the cake or serve n a glass with the cake.

AGA

Place the springform in the middle of the baking oven.
Make the syrup on the boiling plate.
Make the liqueur on the simmering plate.

Tartine russe

FOR 10 PORTIONS

FOR THE BUTTER CREAM:
6 egg yolks
1 egg
2.5 dl water
500 g granulated sugar
600 g butter, at room temperature and in lumps

FOR THE BISCUIT:
300 g butter, at room temperature
300 g fine granulated sugar
1 pinch of salt
300 g of flour

BUTTER CREAM

Beat the egg yolks and the egg till frothy in a food processor with a beater.

Bring the water and sugar to the boil and reduce until the sugar syrup has reached 120 °C.

Leave the food processor running and trickle the sugar syrup into the eggs.

Add the butter and beat into a smooth mass.

Place in a piping bag with a serrated piping mouth and leave in the refrigerator.

BISCUIT

Pre-heat the oven to 180 °C.

Beat the butter, sugar and salt in a food processor with a beater.

Fold in the flour, a spoonful at a time, and mix till smooth.

Place a sheet of baking paper or a baking mat on a 40 x 30 cm baking tray.

Spread a thin, even layer of mixture over the baking tray with a palette knife.

Bake for 8 to 9 minutes in the pre-heated oven until golden brown.

Immediately cut the biscuit into 20 equal pieces with a sharp knife.

Pipe tufts of butter cream on 10 biscuits and place the other halves on top of them, bottom side up. Press gently together.

AGA

Place the baking tray in the middle of the baking oven.

TIP

Cut the biscuits very quickly after baking, because the it stiffens very quickly and then cannot be cut.

BREAD

Ode to home-made bread straight from the oven

Freshly baked bread just out of the oven - doesn't it at once put you into a good mood? Although the image of bread has deteriorated somewhat, there are also many healthy variants. On top of that, bread is an all-rounder that you can use for snacks as well as the main part of the meal. Use the recipes in this book to conjure up onto the table breads packed with flavour and attractive to the eye.

FOR AN 17 x 17 CM SQUARE SPRINGFORM

4 bananas (300 g), peeled
10 g baking powder
400 g wheat flour
pinch of salt
2 eggs
125 g sugar
butter for greasing the baking tin
flour to dust baking tin

Banana bread

Pre-heat the oven to 170 °C.

Purée the bananas and mix with the baking powder, flour, salt, eggs and sugar in a food processor using a dough hook. Knead into a homogeneous dough.

Place the dough in a buttered springform and cover with baking paper.

Bake for 30 minutes in the pre-heated oven.

Remove the baking paper and bake for another 20 minutes in the oven.

Remove the bread from the tin and leave on a wire rack to cool.

AGA

Bake the bread on a grid on the bottom of the baking oven.

FOR 4 ROLLS

4 pre-baked rolls
4 slices of smoked ham
60 g Gruyère cheese, grated
pepper
4 eggs
leaves of 2 sprigs of thyme
pinch of paprika
handful of mixed salad

Breakfast pistolets

Pre-heat the oven to 170 °C.

Bake the rolls according to the instructions on the package and leave on a wire rack to cool.

Place a sheet of baking paper or a baking mat on a baking tray.

Cut off the tops of the rolls and scoop them out.

Arrange the rolls on the baking tray and fill them with the ham and cheese. Season with pepper.

Break an egg in the centre of each roll and season with thyme and paprika.

Bake in the pre-heated oven for 10 minutes or until the eggs are cooked.

Serve hot with mixed salad.

AGA

Place the baking tray on the bottom of the baking oven.

FOR A 20 x 20 CM
BAKING TIN

FOR THE YEAST STARTER:
2 teaspoons dry yeast
10 dl lukewarm milk
20 g sugar
75 g wheat flour

FOR THE DOUGH:
225 g wheat flour
30 g sugar
pinch of salt
60 g butter, melted and cooled
1 egg, beaten
1 tablespoon corn oil
60 g light brown sugar
2 teaspoons cinnamon powder
1 egg yolk, beaten
1 can dulce de leche

Brioche oven dish with dulce de leche

YEAST STARTER
Dissolve the yeast in the lukewarm milk and mix in the sugar and wheat flour. Cover with cling foil and leave to rise for 1 hour.

DOUGH
Mix the wheat flour, sugar and salt in a food processor with a dough hook. Add the yeast starter, butter and egg and knead for 4 minutes. Cover and leave to rise for 15 minutes.

Knead for another 3 minutes. Ball up and then roll the dough through the corn oil in a mixing bowl, cover and leave to rise for 90 minutes.

Pre-heat the oven to 180 °C.

Mix the light brown sugar with the cinnamon powder.

Roll out the dough on a floured work surface into a 45 x 25-centimetre rectangle. Sprinkle with the sugar and cinnamon mixture and roll up the dough from the long side.

Cut the ends of the roll off at right angles and cut the roll into 12 equal slices.

Arrange side by side on baking paper in a rectangular baking pan. Cover and leave to rise for one hour.

Brush the dough with the egg yolk. Cover with baking paper.

Bake for 15 minutes in the pre-heated oven.

Remove the baking paper and bake for 20 minutes in the baking oven until the upper side is golden brown.

Heat the dulce de leche and pour over the buns.

AGA

Place the baking tray in the middle of the baking oven. Heat the dulce de leche in the slow cooking oven.

You can make dulce de leche yourself. Place one or more cans of condensed milk in the bottom of a saucepan with plenty of water. Bring the water to the boil and leave to simmer for 3 hours. Make sure that the can is always under water and top up if necessary. Remove the can from the water and leave to cool completely. Open the can and store the dulce de leche in a sealable jar in the refrigerator. Shorten the cooking time to 2 or 2.5 hours if you want the dulce de leche to be less firm.

With the AGA you use the simmering plate or the ovens. Pour the contents of one or more cans of condensed milk into an oven dish and cover well with aluminium foil. Place this oven dish inside a larger oven dish or roasting pan and fill halfway with water. Place the dishes in the top of the slow cooking oven and cook au bain-marie until you obtain a dulce de leche. Keep an eye on the water level and top up if necessary. After an hour and a half, check the colour and consistency of the dulce de leche every 15 minutes. Once you have the result you want, remove the dishes from the oven and leave to cool slightly. Stir the dulce de leche well and store in a sealable jar in the refrigerator.

FOR 1 LOAF
15 g fresh yeast
4.5 dl lukewarm water
750 g white bread flour
10 g butter, at room temperature
15 g salt
200 g red pesto
200 g mozzarella
leaves of 4 sprigs of thyme
pinch of cayenne pepper

Pesto roll

Mix the flour, the dissolved yeast, butter and salt in a food processor with a dough hook and knead for 15 minutes.

Place the dough on a floured work surface, cover with a damp cloth and leave for 15 minutes to rise.

Knead the dough briefly by hand and make into a ball. Cover with a damp cloth and leave to rise for 15 minutes.

Knead again briefly, make into a ball, cover with a damp cloth and leave to rise for 40 minutes.

Pre-heat the oven to 220 ° C and place a bowl of water in the oven.

Bake the bread for 30 minutes in the pre-heated oven.

Open the oven door ajar and bake for another 15 minutes.

Leave the bread to cool completely on a wire rack.

Place a sheet of baking paper or a baking mat on a baking tray.

Lower the oven temperature to 200 °C.

Cut loaf half way down in a grid shape with a knife.

Push the pesto and mozzarella into the cuts. Sprinkle with the thyme and season with the cayenne pepper.

Bake in the pre-heated oven for maximum 10 minutes until the cheese has melted.

Remove from oven and serve as finger food for sharing.

AGA

Place a bowl of water on the bottom of the roasting oven and bake the bread for 50 minutes. Do not open the door.
Bake the bread on the bottom of the roasting oven for the last stage until the cheese has melted.

FOR 1 LOAF
10 g dry yeast
1.5 dl lukewarm water
120 g sugar
pinch of salt
olive oil
350 g wheat flour, sifted
leaves of 2 sprigs of rosemary, finely chopped
300 g seedless rosé grapes
icing sugar for decoration

Grape bread

Dissolve the yeast in the water and leave for 5 minutes.

Mix 60 grams of sugar with the salt in a mixing bowl. Make a well and pour in the dissolved yeast and 2 tablespoons olive oil. Now mix the flour into the liquid little by little.

Remove onto a floured work surface and knead into a smooth dough.

Place the dough into an oiled mixing bowl, cover and leave to rise for one hour.

Pre-heat the oven to 200 °C.

Place a sheet of baking paper or a baking mat on a baking tray.

Roll out the dough into a rectangular piece and place it on the baking tray.

Brush with olive oil, sprinkle with the rosemary needles and lightly push the grapes into the dough.

Sprinkle with the rest of the sugar.

Bake for 30 minutes in the pre-heated oven.

Decorate with icing sugar.

AGA

Place the baking plate at the top of the baking oven.

FOR 8 ROLLS

FOR THE FLATBREAD:
20 g fresh yeast
250 g lukewarm water
1 teaspoon honey
500 g wheat flour, sifted
1 teaspoon salt
4 tablespoons olive oil
1 tablespoon corn oil
½ teaspoon dried rosemary
½ teaspoon fennel seeds
1 teaspoon dried basil

FOR THE AVOCADO SPREAD:
2 shallots, peeled and shredded
4 tomatoes, peeled and diced
4 tablespoons olive oil
1 tablespoon red wine vinegar
pepper and salt
4 avocados
juice of ½ lemon
pinch of salt
pinch of cayenne pepper
1 clove garlic, peeled and shredded
250 g ricotta
2 tablespoons finely chopped chives
16 basil leaves

Flatbread with avocado spread

FLATBREAD

Dissolve the yeast in the water and add the honey. Mix in 2 tablespoons wheat flour and leave for 15 minutes.

Add the rest of the wheat flour, salt and olive oil and knead for 5 minutes in a food processor with a dough hook to form an elastic dough.

Make into a ball, roll the dough through the corn oil in a mixing bowl, cover with a damp cloth and leave to rise for 1 hour until the dough has doubled in volume.

Pre-heat the oven to 240 °C.

Knead the rosemary, fennel seeds and basil into the dough.

Divide the dough into 8 pieces and roll out into slices.

Place a sheet of baking paper or a baking mat on a baking tray.

Bake for 5 to 6 minutes in the pre-heated oven.

Place on a wire rack to cool.

AVOCADO SPREAD

Mix the shallot, tomato, olive oil and red wine vinegar into a vinaigrette and season with salt and pepper.

Cut the avocados in half, remove the stone and peel the flesh.

Mash the avocado with a fork and drizzle with the lemon juice. Season with salt and cayenne pepper. Mix with the garlic, ricotta and chives.

Bake the breads in a hot grill pan, spread with the avocado spread and finish with basil leaves. Serve with the vinaigrette.

AGA

Place the baking tray on the bottom of the roasting oven.

TIP

You can easily remove the pulp of avocados with a spoon.
Always use dried herbs in bread dough.

FOR 1 LOAF

FOR THE DOUGH:
- 7 g dry yeast
- 120 g whole milk, lukewarm
- 50 g sugar
- 375 g wheat flour
- 2 eggs
- 60 g butter, melted
- 7 g of salt

FOR THE FILLING:
- 60 g butter, at room temperature
- 150 g light brown caster sugar
- 2 teaspoons cinnamon powder

Luxury bread with sweet cinnamon filling

Dissolve the yeast in the milk and add the sugar.

Mix the flour, eggs, butter, salt and dissolved yeast in a food processor with a dough hook and knead for 5 minutes.

Place the dough on a floured work surface. Make into a ball, cover and leave to rise for one hour.

Roll out the dough into a 30 x 40 centimetre rectangle.

Mix the butter, the light brown caster sugar and the cinnamon powder for the filling and spread over the dough.

Roll up the dough. Cut the dough lengthwise into two strips and braid them together.

Place the dough in a baking or cake tin, cover with a damp cloth and leave for hour to rise.

Pre-heat the oven to 170 °C.

Cover the bread with baking paper and bake for 20 minutes in the pre-heated oven.

Remove the baking paper and bake for 15 minutes in the oven.

Remove the bread from the tin and leave on a wire rack to cool.

AGA

Place the baking or cake tin on the bottom of the baking oven.

FOR 1 LOAF
8 g dry yeast
3.3 dl lukewarm water
600 g flour, sifted
2 teaspoons cumin powder
2 teaspoons dried coriander powder
2 teaspoons paprika
2 tablespoons argan oil
2 teaspoons salt
2 cloves garlic, peeled and pressed
130 g red pesto
3 tablespoons harissa

Morrocan bread

Dissolve the yeast in the water.

Mix the sifted flour, dissolved yeast, cumin powder, coriander powder, paprika, argan oil and salt in a food processor with a dough hook and knead for 3 minutes into a smooth dough.

Cover and leave to rise for one hour.

Pre-heat the oven to 180 °C.

Place a sheet of baking paper or a baking mat on a baking tray.

Roll out the dough to 45 x 60 centimetres rectangle.

Mix the garlic with the red pesto and the harissa and spread over the dough.

Roll up the dough from a longer side and place on the baking tray. Score the roll with a sharp knife.

Bake for 45 minutes in the pre-heated oven.

AGA

Place the baking tray in the middle of the baking oven.

FOR 40 ROLLS

20 g fresh yeast
5 dl lukewarm water
200 g brown bread flour
20 g salt
575 g wheat flour
250 g mixed nuts, roughly chopped

Nut rolls

Dissolve the yeast in the water.

Place the brown bread flour and the salt in the mixing bowl of a food processor with a dough hook and sift the wheat flour over it. Add the dissolved yeast with the nuts and knead into an elastic dough.

Place the dough onto a floured work surface and knead for again 5 minutes.

Make into a ball, cover with a damp cloth and leave to rise for 45 to 60 minutes until doubled in volume.

Place a sheet of baking paper or a baking mat on a baking tray.

Make balls of 35 grams, roll them into baguettes, arrange them on the baking tray, cover and leave to rise for 30 minutes.

Pre-heat the oven to 180 °C.

Sift some flour over the rolls.

Bake for 20 minutes in the pre-heated oven.

AGA

Place the baking tray in the middle of the baking oven.

TIP

These rolls can easily be stored in the freezer.

FOR 2 LOAVES
- 20 g fresh yeast
- 3.5 dl lukewarm water
- 1 tablespoon honey
- 500 g spelt flour
- 1 teaspoon salt
- 8 stewing pears peeled and halved
- 5 dl sweet white wine
- 300 g Roquefort, crumbled
- 8 sprigs thyme
- 4 tablespoons olive oil

Pear and roquefort bread

Dissolve the yeast in the water and add the honey.

Mix the spelt flour with the salt and add the dissolved yeast.

Place the dough onto a floured work surface and knead 10 minutes into a supple, elastic dough.

Make into a ball, place in a mixing bowl, cover and leave to rise for one hour.

Pre-heat the oven to 200 °C.

Stew the pears in the white wine in a covered pan.

Place a sheet of baking paper or a baking mat on a baking tray.

Divide the dough into two halves and shape each piece into a flat loaf. Arrange the loaves on the baking tray.

Bake for 10 minutes in the pre-heated oven.

Remove the loaves from the oven and Spread the pears and ricotta over them

Bake for 5 minutes in the oven.

Decorate with sprigs of thyme and drizzle with olive oil.

AGA

Stew the pears on the simmering plate.
Bake the loaves on the bottom of the roasting oven.

FOR 1 LOAF

25 g fresh yeast
200 g lukewarm milk
300 g flour
15 g white caster sugar
50 g butter
6 g salt
pinch of cinnamon powder
190 g pearl sugar
1 egg yolk, beaten

Sugar loaf

Dissolve the yeast in the milk.

Mix the flour, the dissolved yeast, caster sugar, butter, salt and cinnamon powder in a food processor with a dough hook and knead for 5 minutes.

Place the dough on a floured work surface, make into a ball, cover with a damp cloth and leave to rise for least 1 hour.

Roll out the dough into a thick piece and sprinkle the pearl sugar over it. Fold the dough inwards and make into a ball.

Place the dough into a baking tin lined with baking paper, cover with a damp cloth and leave to rise for 30 minutes.

Pre-heat the oven to 170 °C.

Brush the dough with the beaten egg yolk.

Bake for 30 minutes in the pre-heated oven.

Remove from the mould and leave on a wire rack to cool.

AGA

Place the baking tin on the bottom of the baking oven.

FOR 9 ROLLS

11 g dry yeast
250 g lukewarm water
20 g honey
420 g wheat flour
4 g salt
30 g corn oil
1 tablespoon za'atar
1 egg yolk, beaten
1 teaspoon flake salt

Za'atar rolls

Dissolve the yeast in the water and add the honey.

Mix the flour, the dissolved yeast, salt and corn oil in a food processor with a dough hook and knead for least 6 minutes.

Place the dough on a floured work and roll into a ball. Cover with a damp cloth and leave to rise for 30 minutes.

Roll out the dough to 20 x 30 centimetres rectangle and sprinkle with the za'atar.

Cut into 9 equal strips, roll up each strip and arrange in an oven dish or baking tin.

Brush the rolls with the beaten egg yolk and sprinkle with flake salt.

Cover with a damp cloth and leave to rise for 30 minutes.

Pre-heat the oven to 180 °C.

Bake for 20 to 25 minutes in the pre-heated oven.

AGA

Place the oven dish or baking tin on the bottom of the baking oven.

KATRIEN CALLEWAERT

GUEST CHEF HOBBY COOK

When Katrien enters the kitchen, it's like the Italian sun breaks through. "Admittedly, I'm a bit nervous," she says. She has cooked for Claudia before, but cooking in her kitchen is for her something completely different. She's super organized, like a real chef. Once she's going, she goes all out. Katrien works in a very focused way and gives almost professional explanations of how and why she does certain things. Claudia listens carefully and clearly enjoys the passion with which her friend works in the kitchen, which in the meantime fills with the most delicious smells.

How did you get to know Claudia?

'It seems like it was only yesterday, but in the meantime Claudia and I have known each other for over twenty years. We were introduced by a mutual friend and clicked immediately. We certainly have no shortage of subjects for discussion, given our shared passion for good food and entertaining guests. We can also sit and talk very enthusiastically about the aesthetics involved it - how we arrange the tables and serve the dishes. Every year we also go to Milan with the same little group of friends, on a voyage of discovery to trendy culinary addresses. Enjoy!'

How do you describe yourself?

'I work in banking and insurance, but I'm also extremely passionate foodie. Anyone who follows me on Instagram will find mainly photos of my preparations. I love to cook for the children. Then I serve the classics from my own childhood, but I like to give them a creative twist. By now, when I ask them what they would like to eat, they just ask me to prepare one of my "mama dishes".

I'm also very proud that I have recently started creating the plates on which I serve my dishes. I've only just started pottery-making, but my teacher - Pyotr Morf - is my great source of inspiration and he helps me where he can. When I serve my preparations on my own creations, the circle is complete for me! '

What did you base your choice of dishes on?

'With my selection I want to pay tribute to things that are dear to me. The quattro formaggi takes me back to my childhood and the ski trips to San Candido in Northern Italy. The pizzas they bake in their brick oven there are unbelievably delicious! It's those journeys that have shaped me into the Italophile I am today. The turkey ossobuco is my own recipe and a real "mama dish". The tagliatelle with ricotta and pancetta is an ode to Katrien Buyse, who had a butcher's shop in Oostrozebeke. When they closed down, she gave me her "secret" recipe. Whenever I prepare it, I pay homage to her. I hope you'll enjoy it too! '

FOR 2 POTS

3 cloves garlic, peeled and crushed
2 tablespoons olive oil
2 kg of ripe San Marzano tomatoes, peeled and chopped
1 litre of passata
800 g tinned tomatoes
1 teaspoon spaghetti seasoning
4 sprigs oregano
2 bay leaves
8 basil leaves
pepper and salt
1 tablespoon sugar or honey

Basic tomato sauce

Pre-heat the oven to 200 °C.

Fry the garlic briefly in the olive oil in a cast iron pan.

Add the tomatoes, passata, tinned tomatoes, spaghetti herbs, oregano, bay leaf and basil.

Cook for for 25 minutes without a lid in the pre-heated oven.

Season the sauce with salt and pepper and sugar or honey to taste.

Spoon the sauce into 2 jars and close with a lid. Turn the jars upside down to cool.

AGA

Place the cooking pot for 1 hour in the simmering oven.

TO SERVE 4

8 thin fish fillets, 80 g per portion
1 onion, peeled and shredded
2 cloves garlic, peeled and shredded
olive oil
4 sardine fillets in oil, in pieces
2 tablespoons grappa
2 tablespoons breadcrumbs
pepper and salt
125 g mozzarella, grated
1 small bunch of curly parsley, finely chopped
leaves of 1 sprig of oregano, finely chopped
needles from 1 sprig of rosemary, finely chopped
4 tablespoons lemon juice
1 sprig of rosemary
4 bay leaves

Involtini di pesce

Pre-heat the oven to 200 °C.

Cut two of the eight fish fillets into pieces.

Fry the onion and garlic in the olive oil. Add the sliced fish and sardines, cook everything together briefly, and mix well. Deglaze with the grappa, sprinkle with the breadcrumbs and season with salt and pepper. Reserve.

Cut the six remaining fillets in half lengthwise and roll them up.

Arrange them in an oiled oven dish and brush with the fried mixture.

Sprinkle with the mozzarella and season again with pepper and salt.

Mix 5 tablespoons olive oil, parsley, oregano, rosemary needles and lemon juice and season with salt and pepper. Pour over the fish rolls and top with the sprig of rosemary and the bay leaves.

Bake for 20 minutes in the pre-heated oven.

AGA

Fry everything on the simmering plate.
Place the oven dish in the top of the baking oven.

Turkey ossobuco

TO SERVE 4

- 1 kg turkey ossobuco
- pepper and salt
- flower
- 8 tablespoons olive oil
- little flour
- 4 carrots, cleaned and diced
- 2 stalks of celery, cleaned and diced
- 2 cloves garlic, peeled and shredded
- 800 g tinned chopped tomatoes
- 1 large tablespoon tomato paste
- 3 tomatoes, quartered
- 4 sprigs thyme
- zest of 1 lemon
- 2 dl poultry stock
- 4 sprigs curly parsley
- 200 g Parmesan cheese, finely grated
- 10 basil leaves

Pre-heat the oven to 180 °C.

Season the turkey shanks with salt and pepper and flour. Knock off the excess flour.

Brown the shanks in the olive oil in a cast iron pan. Remove the meat from the pan and reserve.

Stew the carrots, celery and garlic in the same pan for a few minutes.

Add the turkey, chopped tomatoes, tomato paste, tomatoes, thyme and half of the lemon zest and moisten with the poultry stock.

Stew for one 1 hour with the lid on in the pre-heated oven.

Season with salt and pepper, finish with the parsley and the remaining lemon zest.

Serve with Parmesan cheese and the basil leaves.

AGA

Stew for 3 hours with the lid on in the slow cooking oven.

TO SERVE 4

FOR THE BASIL BUTTER
125 g butter, at room temperature
2 sun-dried tomatoes in oil, drained and chopped
1 tablespoon chopped basil
pepper and salt

FOR THE PASTA
2 lobsters, boiled and halved
500 g spaghetti
2 tablespoons olive oil
5 dl basic tomato sauce

Pasta pomodoro with lobster in basil butter

BASIL BUTTER
Mix the butter, sun-dried tomatoes and basil, and season with salt and pepper.

Roll up tightly into a sausage in cling film and wrap extra tightly in a sheet of aluminium foil.

Leave to stiffen in the refrigerator.

PASTA
Put the oven on grill setting.

Place the half lobsters cut side up on a baking tray and cover the lobster meat completely with slices of cold basil butter.

Grill for 5 to 8 minutes until the basil butter turns golden brown.

Cook the spaghetti as instructed on the packaging. Drain and reserve some cooking water.

Fry the spaghetti briefly in a wok pan in the olive oil, add some cooking water and the tomato sauce and heat well.

Serve the pasta with pieces of grilled lobster.

AGA

Place the baking plate right at the top of the roasting oven.

TIP

Make the basil butter the day before so that all the flavours can be absorbed.
The basil butter can be kept in the freezer for a month.

Radiatori al 4 formaggi

TO SERVE 4

- 150 g Taleggio cheese, without crust and into pieces
- 150 g mozzarella, in pieces
- 150 g Bel Paese (or other processed cheese such as Parmigiana), without crust and in pieces
- 150 g Gorgonzola, without crust and chopped
- 400 g tinned tomatoes
- 2 dl cream 40%
- 1 teaspoon dried oregano

Pre-heat the oven to 180 °C.

Put the cheeses in an oven dish and leave to melt in the oven without browning. Stir occasionally with a wooden spoon until the cheeses are completely melted.

Bring the tinned tomatoes to the boil with the cream and the oregano over a low heat. Remove the pan from the heat and crush with a fork.

Cook the pasta as instructed on the packaging and drain.

Mix the melted cheese with the tomato sauce.

Mix the sauce into the pasta and serve immediately.

AGA

Place the oven dish in the simmering oven and regularly check.

TIP

Make your own composition of four cheeses or ask your cheese merchant for advice.

TO SERVE 4

- 1 large shallot, peeled and cut into course strips
- ½ fennel, cleaned and cut into coarse strips
- 2 young carrots, cleaned and cut into coarse strips
- 12 cherry tomatoes
- ¼ butternut squash, peeled and cubed
- olive oil
- pepper and salt
- a handful of sage leaves, finely chopped
- 1 tablespoon pumpkin seeds
- pinch of coarse salt
- 40 g salted butter
- 1 clove garlic, peeled
- 4 leaves of sage
- 250 g fresh spaghetti
- 12 small mozzarella balls

Spaghetti with sage butter

Pre-heat the oven to 200 °C.

Place a sheet of baking paper or a baking mat on a baking tray.

Mix the shallot, fennel, carrots, cherry tomatoes and squash cubes with a good splash of olive oil. Season with salt and pepper and spread over the oven tray.

Roast for 20 minutes in the pre-heated oven.

Briefly mix the finely chopped sage and pumpkin seeds in the blender. Season with the coarse salt.

Melt the salted butter with the garlic until the butter turns light brown and add the sage leaves.

Cook the pasta al dente in salted water.

Mix the roasted vegetables into the pasta and add 2 tablespoons of cooking water. Pour over the sage butter and finish with the mozzarella balls and the pumpkin seed crumble.

AGA

Place the oven tray on the bottom of the roasting oven.

TO SERVE 4

- 500 g tagliatelle
- 3 large onions, peeled and shredded
- 5 cloves garlic, peeled and shredded
- 2 tablespoons olive oil
- 400 g pancetta, finely chopped
- 1 litre of culinary cream
- 400 g tinned chopped tomatoes
- 400 g passata
- 250 g ricotta
- pepper and salt

Tagliatelle with ricotta and pancetta

Pre-heat the oven to 180 °C.

Cook the pasta al dente and drain.

Fry the onion and garlic in the olive oil. Add the pancetta and allow to cook for a while longer.

Place in an oven dish with the pasta and pour the cream over it.

Mix the chopped tomatoes and passata until smooth and cover the pasta with it.

Spread little blobs of ricotta over the pasta dish and season with salt and pepper.

Bake for 20 minutes in the pre-heated oven.

AGA

Place the oven dish in the middle of the roasting oven.

DRIES CLOET

GUEST CHEF - TER DUINEN

If we were to gather together all the chefs whom Dries has sent out well-trained into the world over the course of his career, we would need a very large space indeed. Which is not surprising: Dries has been teaching the 1st and 7th grades at the Hotelschool Ter Duinen in Koksijde for years. He is also one of the driving forces behind Auguste, the school's travelling pop-up restaurant. As well as which, original culinary projects bubble up one after another in his head, and in that of his wife Marieke. The playful names that the couple always give to them appeal to the imagination at least as much as does passionate way in which Dries narrates, cooks and teaches.

What drives you as a teacher?

'Cooking is a passion, and typical of a passion is that you want to share it with others. It's fascinating for me to teach both 1st and 7th grade, because you see your students start out with a dream and ambition, and in the 7th grade you see again from the front row how during their time at the school they've grown into full-fledged chefs or passionate caterers. In short: hospitality life as it is, and as it has totally captivated me.'

How do you prefer to cook?

My motto: know your classics but keep it simple. As a professional you're generally addicted to Escoffier's classic cuisine. That's how I prepare my classics myself. But it's not necessarily the endlessly long recipes or the combination of large numbers of ingredients that guarantee an excellent dish.

I go for simplicity, pure flavours, locally produced and authentic ingredients, and especially the conviviality around the table! The new project that my wife Marieke and I hope to undertake soon perfectly reflects what I mean by this. With our "Join our Table" ("Tafelgelegenheid In Compagnie") project we shall be inviting people to join us at table for a personal, convivial atmosphere.'

How did you get to know Claudia?

'When I was invited to cook with Claudia at a 600-people event. We got on very well right away, I remember that very well. Preparing risotto with Breydel bacon together under pressure apparently creates a bond, because afterwards we made a cookbook together in collaboration with the Hotelschool. Since then we've remained in touch. '

Which dishes do you want to share with us here?

'Everything that I love myself and that is liked by just about everyone. Accessible preparations that don't require you to be a master chef. Tasty stews and casseroles with few ingredients and lots of flavour! I especially hope you'll enjoy the cooking part of the exercise. And then just put the pan in the middle of the table - there's nothing more convivial than that! '

TO SERVE 4

12 large potatoes, peeled and sliced
olive oil for greasing the oven dish
pepper and salt
1 teaspoon mace
160 g Anne-Marie farm cheese with celery, in 3 mm slices
8 slices of smoked ham
200 g butter, in pieces

Celery gratin Anne-Marie

Pre-heat the oven to 180 °C.

Take one third of the potato slices and place them in a greased oven dish, overlapping them. Season with pepper, salt and mace.

Divide half of the cheese slices over the potatoes.

Take another third of the potato slices and place them on the cheese, overlapping them. Season with pepper, salt and mace.

Spread the ham over the potatoes and then the rest of the cheese slices.

End with the remaining potato slices.

Divide the pieces of butter over the layer of potatoes.

Bake for 40 minutes in the pre-heated oven.

AGA

Place the oven dish in the centre of the baking oven.

TIP

Anne-Marie farmhouse cheese is made with celery in the Beauvoordse Walhoeve by cheese maker Anne-Marie.

TO SERVE 4
1 farm chicken 'en crapaudine'
pepper and salt
chicken seasoning
butter
2 onions, peeled and shredded
8 carrots, cleaned and sliced
2 cloves garlic, peeled and shredded
12 Charlotte potatoes, skin on and quartered lengthwise
sprig of rosemary
2 bay leaves
handful of lamb's lettuce, washed.

Farm chicken crapaudine

Pre-heat the oven to 180 °C.

Season the chicken with pepper and chicken seasoning.

Crust the chicken until golden brown on all sides in a knob of butter.

Place the onion, carrots, garlic and potatoes in a buttered baking tray and arrange the chicken flat on top. Place a few lumps of butter on the chicken and add the rosemary and bay leaf.

Roast for 30 minutes in the pre-heated oven.

Check whether the chicken and vegetables are cooked and leave to roast longer if necessary.

Season with pepper and salt and leave to rest for 10 minutes.

Serve with the lamb's lettuce.

AGA

Fry the chicken golden brown on the boiling plate. Place the oven dish on the bottom of the roasting oven.

TIP

With a chicken 'en crapaudine' the backbone is cut out of the chicken, enabling it to lie completely flat. You can easily do that yourself with poultry shears, or you can ask the poulterer or the butcher.

Meat and vegetable confetti

TO SERVE 4

- 2 orange carrots, cleaned
- 2 yellow carrots, cleaned
- 1 courgette, cleaned
- 1 kohlrabi, cleaned and peeled
- ½ white radish, peeled
- 2 shallots, peeled and shredded
- 3 tablespoons olive oil
- 140 g pearl couscous
- 3 dl vegetable stock
- 400 g mixed minced meat, pork/veal
- 1 clove garlic, peeled and shredded
- 2 dl passata
- pinch of smoked paprika
- 150 g hard cheese, grated
- 4 sprigs curly parsley, finely chopped
- 6 basil leaves

Pre-heat the oven to 200 °C.

Cut small balls from the roots with a Parisian scoop and boil in salted water for 2 minutes.

Cut small balls from the courgette, kohlrabi and white radish with a Parisian scoop.

Fry the half of the shallot in olive oil.

Add the pearl couscous and cook together for a while without browning.

Add the vegetable stock and cook till tender.

Mix the minced meat, the rest of the shallot and the garlic and roll into equal balls.

Fry the balls until golden brown in a knob of butter in a cast iron pan.

Bake for 10 minutes in the pre-heated oven.

Add the vegetable confetti and stir briefly.

Add the passata and bake for 15 minutes in the pre-heated oven.

Add the couscous and season with salt, pepper and the smoked paprika powder.

Finish with the grated cheese, curly parsley and basil.

AGA

Boil the carrot balls on the boiling plate.
Cook the shallot and the pearl couscous on the simmering plate.
Fry the balls on the boiling plate.
Place the oven dish on the bottom of the roasting oven.

TIP

Vary the vegetables as in season to your heart's content.

Mussels thermidor

TO SERVE 4

- 1 onion, peeled and shredded
- butter
- 2 kg mussels, cleaned
- 1 celery stalk, cleaned and chopped
- pepper and salt
- pinch of celery salt
- 1 bottle of Hendrik Geeraert beer (or other top-fermented beer)
- 45 g butter
- 60 g flour
- 1 l milk
- nutmeg
- 1 egg yolk
- 1 dl cream 40%
- 200 g Gruyère cheese, finely grated
- leaves of 4 sprigs curly parsley, finely chopped

Fry the onion in a knob of butter in a large pot.

Add the mussels and celery and season with pepper and celery salt.

Deglaze with a good shot of beer.

Cook the mussels over a high heat with the lid on and shake regularly until the shells open.

Drain the mussels and collect the cooking liquid. Reserve.

Remove the mussels from the shells.

Place the mussels in a buttered oven dish.

Melt the butter in a large saucepan and mix in the flour well. Leave the roux to dry. Add the milk and 1 dl of the cooking water from the mussels while stirring. Bring to the boil and stir vigorously until you get a smooth béchamel sauce. Season with pepper, salt and nutmeg.

Remove from the heat. Beat the egg yolk with the cream and add. Beat well.

Add the grated cheese and stir well until all the cheese has melted.

Put the oven on grill setting.

Add the parsley and divide the sauce over the mussels.

Gratinate under the grill.

AGA

Cook the mussels on the boiling plate.
Make the béchamel sauce on the boiling plate.
Place the oven dish at the top of the roasting oven.

TIP

Freeze the cooking liquid in blocks in the freezer and keep as seasoning.

Oven dish à la Delphine Parmentier

TO SERVE 4

A dish that the kids will really appreciate!

- 1 onion, peeled and shredded
- 1 clove garlic, peeled and crushed
- butter
- 600 g mixed minced meat
- 150 g grated carrots
- 25 g flour
- 4 dl milk
- pepper and salt
- nutmeg
- 400 g mashed potatoes
- 2 tablespoons breadcrumbs

Pre-heat the oven to 175 °C.

Fry the onion and garlic in the butter.

Add the minced meat and cook well.

Place the minced meat into a greased oven dish.

Sprinkle the grated carrots over it.

Melt 20 grams of butter in a large saucepan and mix in the flour well. Leave the roux to dry. Add the milk while stirring. Bring to the boil and stir vigorously until you get a smooth béchamel sauce. Season with pepper, salt and nutmeg.

Spread the béchamel sauce over the oven dish.

Spread the mashed potatoes across the oven dish.

Sprinkle with the breadcrumbs and put a few knobs of butter on top.

Bake for 40 minutes in the pre-heated oven.

AGA

Fry everything on the simmering plate.
Make the béchamel sauce on the boiling plate.
Place the oven dish in the centre of the baking oven.

TO SERVE 4

FOR THE DOUGH
500 g flour
2.4 dl lukewarm water
18 g fresh yeast or 9 g dry yeast
1 egg
5 g salt
2 tablespoons leek oil

FOR THE PIZZA
1 leek, cleaned and chopped
knob of butter
pepper and salt
1 pot of soured cream
1 onion, peeled and finely sliced
100 g smoked bacon
100 g Comté cheese, finely grated
1 tablespoon oregano

Cheese and bacon pizza

Mix all ingredients for the dough in a food processor with a dough hook on medium speed and knead into a smooth, even dough.

Place the dough on a floured wooden board and roll into a ball. Cover with a damp cloth and leave to rise for 30 minutes.

Pre-heat the oven to 250 °C.

Roll out the dough into a nice round pizza base.

Lightly fry the leek in a knob of butter and season with salt and pepper.

Spread the soured cream across the pizza base, keeping 2 centimetres away from the edge.

Top with the fried leek, the onion and the smoked bacon and season with salt and pepper.

Divide the grated cheese over the pizza and sprinkle with oregano.

Bake for 8 minutes in the pre-heated oven.

AGA

Fry the leek on the simmering plate.
Place the pizza on a pizza shovel and bake directly on the bottom of the roasting oven.

TIP

You can easily make leek oil yourself. Cut the green off the leek and let it steep for 30 minutes at 70 degrees in neutral oil. Mix in a blender and strain through a coffee filter. Store in a dark place in a closed bottle.

Lamb tagine

TO SERVE 4

- 900 g of lamb shoulder, boned and cut into chunks
- 4 tablespoons olive oil
- pepper and salt
- 2 merguez sausages
- 2 onions, peeled and roughly chopped
- 1 red onion, peeled and roughly chopped
- 1 sweet pointed pepper + 1 green pepper, seeded and diced
- 1 yellow turnip, peeled and diced
- 10 young carrots, cleaned and cut diagonally
- 2 cloves garlic, peeled and crushed
- 2 teaspoons ras el hanout
- 1 sprig of rosemary
- 2 bay leaves
- 2 sprigs thyme
- 4 sprigs parsley
- 3 dl lamb stock
- ¼ pointed cabbage, cleaned and chopped

Pre-heat the oven to 160 °C.

Colour the lamb in a tagine (earthenware cooking pot) in the olive oil. Season with pepper and salt and reserve.

Fry the merguez in the same tagine. Season with pepper and salt and reserve.

Fry the onion, red onion, pointed pepper, green pepper, yellow turnip, carrots and garlic in the same tagine.

Add the ras el hanout, rosemary, bay leaves, thyme and parsley.

Arrange the lamb and merguez on top of the vegetables and moisten with the lamb stock.

Cover with the lid and cook for 80 minutes in the pre-heated oven.

Add the pointed cabbage and cook for another 10 minutes in the pre-heated oven.

AGA

Place the tagine in the simmering oven.

TIP

Serve this tagine with tabbouleh, couscous, Turkish bread, baguette or pitta bread.

FOR ONE TART
3 eggs
2 cups sugar
1 cup corn oil
1 cup yoghurt
2 cups self-raising flour
2 apples, cored and diced
zest of ½ lime
1 sheet shortcrust pastry
1 tablespoon jam

"Marieke's cups"- yoghurt tart

Pre-heat the oven to 180 °C.

Mix the egg and sugar until frothy with a hand blender.

Add the corn oil and yoghurt and mix well.

Add the flour and mix briefly.

Fold the diced apple into the mixture and add the lime zest.

Place the sheet of shortcrust pastry in a buttered tart mould.

Cover the pastry with baking paper and fill with baking beans.

Blind bake for 15 minutes in the pre-heated oven.

Remove the baking paper and baking beans.

Stir the jam and brush the tart base with it.

Fill the tart base with the yoghurt mixture.

Bake for 25 minutes in the pre-heated oven.

Check whether the filling is done with a knife and bake longer if necessary.

AGA

Place the tart mould in the middle of the baking oven.

TIP

A recipe with cups instead of weighed ingredients is super handy when the kitchen scale batteries fail yet again. In America, by the way, ingredients are usually calculated with cups.

ELLEN DULST

GUEST CHEF - LE FOX

Ellen is well-known as the wife of star chef Stéphane Buyens and the perfect hostess of their restaurant Le Fox in De Panne. However, Ellen is also a gifted chef in her own right. She spent seven years as a pupil at Hotelschool Ter Duinen, which is also reflected in the way she works in the kitchen: meticulously and with every aspect of her preparations under control. While she and Claudia chat away, she keeps a constant eye on the timing and now and then slips away, returning a little later with a broad smile. "It'll be fine!" she says. An understatement that is evident from the dishes she serves shortly afterwards. Delicious!

What's your connection with Claudia?
'We first met in Le Fox, when we had Claudia and Kurt as guests to dinner with us. We clicked immediately. We started talking and we also invited each other privately. When Claudia took part in the programme The Best Hobby Chef I followed her closely, of course, I was a fan! '

Who cooks at home?
'In Le Fox I've been the perfect team with Stéphane for twenty years. We sense each other and the division of tasks is very simple: he's the cook and I'm the hostess. At home I'm mainly the mother and wife who enjoys cooking tasty, healthy food for her family. Stéphane is delighted to come home and simply sit down at table with Eloise, our 14-year-old daughter. When we invite guests to our home, we take turns: sometimes he cooks, sometimes I do. We both still cook with lots of passion. I personally find it very important to prepare everything well so that we can have aperitifs together with our guests and then sit down at the table.'

Your favourite cooking style?
'I go for light dishes that do full justice to the purity of the ingredients. That's why I mainly work on taste and with lots of vegetables. For example, you won't see me using heavier ingredients like cheese. In the past that was definitely not the case, but I experienced more and more that "heavy" feeling, a sort of dip, after eating. I like to be active and reasonably sporty, but without exaggerating. The way I cook now simply fits in much better with my current lifestyle.'

Which dishes have you selected for us?
'In line with how I prefer to cook: especially oven dishes! Without cheese and without cream, but full of flavour. Of course I've also been "shaped" by the top ingredients I see Stéphane using at Le Fox. Sometimes I get itchy fingers and can't wait to get into the kitchen at home and give it my own twist. However, the fact that I like to cook light and healthy doesn't mean I don't enjoy a sweet treat every now and then. That is why I definitely wanted to include the recipe for my pear frangipane. Enjoy!'

TO SERVE 4

FOR THE DOUGH
180 g sugar
180 g ground almonds
140 g butter, at room temperature
3 eggs, at room temperature
pinch of salt
250 g flour

FOR THE PEARS
2 large ripe pears
40 g flaked almonds
1.5 dl milk
160 g dark chocolate, broken into pieces
vanilla ice cream

Pear frangipane

FRANGIPANE
Mix the sugar, ground almonds, butter, eggs, salt and half of the flour in the food processor.

Add the remaining flour and mix to a smooth dough.

PEAR
Pre-heat the oven to 220 °C.

Halve the pears and cut a slice from the bottom to prevent them from falling over.

Remove the core with an ice cream scoop. Using the same ice cream scoop, scoop a portion of frangipane dough and fill the hollow with it.

Sprinkle with flaked almonds.

Place a sheet of baking paper in an oven dish and place the pears on top.

Bake for 50 minutes in the pre-heated oven.

Check if the frangipane is cooked and remove from the oven.

Bring the milk to the boil and pour over the pure chocolate. Stir until all the chocolate has melted and add a splash of lukewarm water if the sauce is too thick.

Serve the pear with a scoop of vanilla ice cream and the chocolate sauce.

AGA
Place the oven dish in the top of the baking oven. Boil the milk on the boiling plate.

TO SERVE 4

- 8 waxy potatoes, peeled
- 4 tablespoons grape seed oil
- 2 large red onions, peeled and sliced
- 1 fennel, trimmed, cut into halves and then into rings, stems separately
- 2 tablespoons olive oil + extra for greasing oven dish
- pepper and salt
- 2 lemons, with both skin and white pith removed and thickly sliced
- 4 pieces of thick cod fillet, 200 g each
- 4 bay leaves
- leaves of 8 sprigs flat parsley, finely chopped

Cod boulangère

Pre-heat the oven to 200 °C.

Cut the potatoes into fine slices with a mandolin slicer. Rinse under cold running water and drain.

Bake the potato slices in the oven for 5 minutes. Add the red onion and the fennel and drizzle with the olive oil.

Leave to simmer 10 minutes and stir regularly. Season with pepper and salt.

Divide the potatoes, onion, fennel and lemons over a greased oven dish.

Season the cod with salt and pepper and arrange on top of the vegetables in the oven dish.

Add the bay leaves and sprinkle with some finely chopped fennel leaves and flat parsley.

Drizzle with some olive oil.

Bake for 20 minutes in the pre-heated oven.

Garnish with some fennel and flat parsley.

AGA

Stew the vegetables on the simmering plate.
Place the oven dish on the bottom of the roasting oven.

TIP

This recipe can be perfectly prepared the day before. Place covered in the refrigerator and extend the cooking time by 10 minutes.

TO SERVE 4

- 1 kg minced chicken
- pepper and salt
- 8 dl poultry stock
- 16 Brussels sprouts, cleaned
- 8 dl vegetable stock
- 6 carrots, cleaned and sliced
- 2 leek stems, cleaned and in rings
- 1 large turnip, peeled and sliced
- 1 yacón (Peruvian ground apple), cleaned and sliced
- 500 g Parisian mushrooms, cleaned and cut in half
- ½ bunch of curly parsley, finely chopped

Chicken balls in Flanders fields

Pre-heat the oven to 180 °C.

Season the minced chicken with pepper and salt and roll equal balls.

Bring the poultry stock to the boil with 4 dl water and cook the meatballs for 10 to 15 minutes.

Leave the balls to cool in the cooking liquid.

Cook the Brussels sprouts in salted water and immediately place in ice-cold water. Reserve.

Bring the vegetable stock to the boil with 4 dl of water and cook the carrots, leek, turnip, yacón and mushrooms until half done. Drain and reserve the cooking liquid.

Place the meatballs and vegetables into an oven dish. Add half the chicken stock and half the vegetable stock until the balls are covered.

Cook in the pre-heated oven for 20 minutes until everything is hot.

Serve in soup plates and finish with the finely chopped parsley.

AGA

Cook the vegetables on the boiling plate.
Place the oven dish in the centre of the baking oven.

Spring chickens Brabançonne

TO SERVE 4

- 8 heads of Belgian endive, cleaned
- butter
- 4 dl vegetable stock
- 16 new potatoes, washed
- patatas bravas herbs
- 4 spring chickens 'en crapaudine' (p. 285)
- 2 large shallots, peeled and shredded
- 12 slices of smoked bacon, cut into strips
- salt and pepper
- 2 + 2 dl poultry stock
- 4 sprigs rosemary

Pre-heat the oven to 180 °C.

Colour the Belgian endive all over in a knob of butter, add the vegetable stock and cook with the lid on a low heat.

Cook the potatoes until tender. Drain and fry until golden brown with a knob of butter. Season with the patatas bravas herbs.

Colour the spring chickens golden brown all round in a generous pat of butter. Season with pepper and salt. Add the shallot and bacon and cook together briefly.

Add 2 dl of chicken stock and cook for 15 minutes with the lid on.

Place the Belgian endive in a buttered oven dish. Divide the potatoes, spring chickens, bacon and shallot over the oven dish.

Deglaze the pan with the spring chickens with 2 dl of poultry stock and scrape off the burnt residues. Spread over the oven dish and add the rosemary.

Bake for 35 minutes in the pre-heated oven.

AGA

Cook the Belgian endive on the simmering plate.
Bring the potatoes to the boil on the boiling plate, drain and cook, with the lid on, in the centre of the slow cooking oven for 20 minutes.
Fry the spring chickens on the boiling plate until golden brown and cook, with the lid on, on the bottom of the roasting oven.
Place the oven dish in the centre of the baking oven.

TO SERVE 4

- 1 kg minced veal
- 2 large shallots, peeled and shredded
- 2 eggs
- pepper and salt
- butter
- 2 tablespoons grape seed oil
- 2 large shallots, quartered with skin
- 4 dl veal stock
- 20 cherry tomatoes in different colours
- 2 courgettes, cleaned and roughly chopped
- 1 yellow pointed pepper, seeded and roughly chopped
- 1 red pointed pepper, seeded and roughly chopped
- 1 bok choy, roughly chopped
- 800 g passata
- 1 teaspoon dried oregano
- 20 basil leaves

Mediterranean meat loaf

Pre-heat the oven to 220 °C.

Mix the minced veal, shallot and eggs in the food processor or with your hands. Season with pepper and salt and form a loaf.

Place the loaf in a buttered oven dish. Drizzle with the grape seed oil and add the peeled shallot wedges.

Bake for 20 minutes in the pre-heated oven.

Add the veal stock and bake for 15 minutes in the pre-heated oven.

Remove the oven dish from the oven and lower the temperature to 180 °C.

Add the cherry tomatoes, courgette, yellow and red peppers, bok choy, passata and oregano and season with salt and pepper.

Bake for 15 minutes in the pre-heated oven.

Cut the meat loaf into thick slices and garnish with the basil leaves.

AGA

Place the oven dish in the middle of the roasting oven. Place the oven dish with the vegetables in the middle of the baking oven.

EDDY NOPPE

GUEST CHEF - PASTRYCOOK

Eddy's story is one of a little boy growing up in a hard-working West Flemish confectionery baker's family, in which love for the profession passed from one generation to the next. The story of a craft as the focus of daily life, in which the romance of tarts and cakes created with fresh fruit, dark chocolate and praline did not escape Eddy's attention when he saw customers' eyes light up in the bakery shop window.

From where the passion for confectionery baking?

'My father was a confectionery baker through and through. In 1953 he started his own bakery in Harelbeke, Patisserie Noppe. As a boy of about twelve, I was already spending much of my free time helping out in the bakery kitchen. Weekends, evenings after school, during the holidays... you were more likely to find me in the bakery than behind my textbooks. No one was surprised when I too opted for the profession. In 1983 I finally took over my father's business completely. We did good business. At one point we were eight to ten bakers in our bakery kitchen, and well-known restaurants, banqueting halls and wedding caterers came knocking on our door at Harelbeke. In the meantime, since 2012 I'm "retired", as they say. I don't bake much at home any more, but I'm happy to make an exception for Claudia.'

How did you get to know Claudia?

'Of course I knew who Claudia was, but I'd never spoken to her in person. Until there was a photo shoot with mutual friends of ours for the book Claudia Feest. Then we got talking. The respect was mutual and we kept in touch. Now we often see each other at those friends' house by the sea, and then catch up on a terrace or with a group on the beach. It's nice to be able to make a small contribution to this book in my turn!'

What type of pastry makes you happy?

'I am and will remain an upholder of traditional pastries. We were known for our fruit cakes, chocolate cakes, bonbons... Not to mention the ice cream cakes, which used to be a real tradition for holidays and special occasions. I like pure flavours, pure ingredients. So you won't see me experimenting in a hurry. What I do pay a lot of attention to and in which I dare to be creative, is the presentation. The eye wants something too; I like a modern, original design.'

Which dishes have you selected for us, and why?

'Most of what I've chosen starts with puff pastry. A delicious pear pie, appetizers with puff pastry... Recipes that everyone can manage, not too complicated but full of flavour. For me it's important to put a delicious cake or tart on the table that you're almost certain the whole family will enjoy. No "specials" in terms of ingredients or recipe, but the delicious, traditional cake or tart that grandma used to bake on Sundays and that everyone looked forward to.'

1000 g flour
450 g of water
20 g salt
150 g butter
500 g butter for rolling out,
at room temperature

Basic recipe puff pastry

Mix the flour, water, salt and 150 grams of butter with a food processor or with your hands and knead into a smooth and supple dough.

Roll out the dough into a rectangular shape.

Place the 500 grams of butter on two thirds of the rolled-out dough and fold in three.

Roll out again into a rectangle and fold into thirds.

Leave for at least 1 hour in the refrigerator.

Roll out a third time into a rectangle and fold in thirds.

Roll out a fourth time into a rectangle and fold into thirds.

Leave for at least 1 hour in the refrigerator.

Roll out a fifth time into a rectangle and fold in thirds.

Roll out a sixth time into a rectangle and fold into thirds.

Leave for at least 1 hour in the refrigerator.

The puff pastry is now ready for use and can be kept refrigerated and packaged for 4 to 5 days.

FOR A Ø 20 CM RING

FOR THE CREME PATISSIERE
7.5 + 2.5 dl whole milk
110 + 40 g granulated sugar
contents of 1 vanilla pod
6 egg yolks
125 g cornflour

FOR THE BASE
1 round sheet of puff pastry,
Ø 28 cm, rolled out 1.5 mm
thick

FOR THE CHIPOLATA CRÈME
1 sheet of gelatine
300 g crême pâtissière
100 g cream 40%
15 g icing sugar

FOR THE DECORATION
2 tablespoons apricot jam
1 tin of pears in light syrup
(425 g)
70 g flaked almonds, toasted
icing sugar for finishing

Burned pear tart

CREME PATISSIERE

Bring 7.5 dl of milk, 100 g of sugar and the vanilla to the boil.

Beat the egg yolks and 40 g sugar until fluffy in a food processor.

Beat the cornflour in 2.5 dl milk and mix with the egg yolks.

Pour this mixture into the boiling milk and bring to the boil again, stirring constantly until a good binding is formed.

Pour the crême pâtissière into a shallow dish and immediately cover with cling film.

Leave to cool as fast as possible and place in the refrigerator.

BASE

Pre-heat the oven to 180 °C.

Place a sheet of baking paper or a baking mat on a baking tray and place a Ø 20 centimetre stainless steel ring on top.

Cover the ring with the puff pastry and press firmly against the ring. Push off the excess dough and even the edges between your thumb and forefinger.

Leave for 5 minutes in the freezer to stiffen.

Cover the pastry with baking paper and fill with baking beans.

Blind bake for 15 minutes in the pre-heated oven.

Remove the baking paper and baking beans.

Bake for 5 to 10 minutes in the pre-heated oven until golden brown and crispy.

Remove from the oven and leave on a wire rack to cool.

Remove the ring.

CHIPOLATA CRÈME

Soak the gelatine sheet in cold water, squeeze and melt over a low heat in a pan.

Beat the crème pâtissière until smooth and add the melted gelatine.

Beat the cream with the icing sugar and fold into the crème pâtissière.

Place the crème into a piping bag.

FINISHING

Brush the base with boiled apricot jam.

Fill the mould one third full with the chipolata crème.

Cover the tart two-thirds up with the pears.

Fill to the brim with chipolata crème.

Cover the top completely with the toasted flaked almonds.

Sprinkle with a thick layer of icing sugar and burn off with a Bunsen burner.

AGA

Place the baking tray on the bottom of the baking oven.

FOR 40 BISCUITS
2 rectangular sheets of puff pastry, 40 x 25 cm, rolled out to a thickness of approx. 3 mm
1 egg yolk, beaten

FOR THE CHEESE SAUCE
4 + 1 dl milk
45 g cornflour
4 egg yolks
pepper and salt
nutmeg
325 g Gruyère cheese, finely grated

FOR THE DECORATION
walnuts, shrimps, extra grated Gruyère

Cheese biscuits

BISCUITS
Pre-heat the oven to 180 °C.

Place a sheet of baking paper or a baking mat on a baking tray.

Cut out rounds of puff pastry with a cutting ring of about 4 centimetres diameter.

Arrange half of the rounds on the baking tray and brush with beaten egg yolk.

Cut circles again from the other half with a smaller ring of about 3.5 centimetres.

Remove the round, which is excess dough.

Arrange the rings on the rounds on the baking tray. Briefly press together with a flat object.

Brush the edges with beaten egg yolk.

Bake for 10 minutes in the pre-heated oven.

Leave to cool.

CHEESE SAUCE
Bring 4 dl milk to the boil.

Beat the cornflour, egg yolks and 1 dl milk with a beater and season with salt, pepper and nutmeg.

Add to the boiling milk and beat into a smooth, solid mass.

Remove from the heat and add the grated cheese. Stir until all the cheese has melted.

Leave to cool in the refrigerator.

Pre-heat the oven to 180 °C.

Stir the cheese cream loosely with a whisk and place it in a piping bag.

Pipe the cheese cream into the puff pastry cups.

Finish with walnuts, shrimps and grated cheese as you like.

Bake for 8 to 10 minutes in the pre-heated oven just before serving.

AGA

Place the baking tray in the middle of the baking oven. Make the béchamel sauce on the boiling plate. Place the baking tray the second time round on the bottom of the baking oven.

TIP

The puff pastry biscuits are also available ready-made in shops.

Kilometre tart with fresh fruit

FOR ONE TART

FOR THE BASE
1 rectangular sheet of puff pastry 10 x 25 cm, rolled out to a thickness of 1.5 mm
2 strips of puff pastry, 1 x 25 cm, rolled out to a thickness of 1.5 mm

FOR THE CREME PATISSIERE
7.5 + 2.5 dl whole milk
110 + 40 g granulated sugar
contents of 1 vanilla pod
6 egg yolks
125 g cornflour

FOR THE DECORATION
30 raspberries
icing sugar
3 sprigs red berries
12 blueberries
12 blackberries
2 slices of fresh pineapple, chopped
6 strawberries, halved
a few leaves of mint
4 leaves of edible gold (optional)

BASE
Place a sheet of baking paper or a baking mat on a baking tray.

Place the rectangular piece of puff pastry on the baking tray.

Place the bands of puff pastry left and right on the edges of the rectangular piece of puff pastry and press well.

Leave for at least 3 hours to prevent deformation.

Pre-heat the oven to 180 °C.

Make a few notches in the outer edge of the dough with a fork or with your fingers.

Bake for 15 minutes in the pre-heated oven.

Place on a wire rack to cool.

CREME PATISSIERE
Bring 7.5 dl of milk, 100 g of sugar and the vanilla to the boil.

Beat the egg yolks and 40 grams sugar until fluffy in a food processor.

Dissolve the cornflour in 2.5 dl of milk and mix with the egg yolks.

Pour this mixture into the boiling milk and bring to the boil again, stirring constantly until a good binding is formed.

Pour the crème pâtissière into a shallow dish and immediately cover with cling film.

Leave to cool as fast as possible and place in the refrigerator.

FINISHING
Beat the crème pâtissière lightly and place into a piping bag.

Pipe a layer of crème patissière onto the base.

Arrange the raspberries around the edge and sprinkle with the icing sugar.

Arrange the rest of the fruit between the raspberries and finish with the edible gold.

AGA

Place the baking plate at the top of the baking oven.

FOR 12 TOASTS

FOR THE TOASTS
1 rectangular sheet of of puff pastry, 40 x 25 cm, rolled out to a thickness of approx. 3 mm

FOR THE SMOKED SALMON
6 g gelatine sheets
100 g smoked salmon for the mousse
90 + 35 g fish fumet
125 g cream 40%, half beaten
1 tablespoon ketchup
4 drops of Tabasco
a few sprigs of dill
pepper and salt
2 slices of smoked salmon

Toasts with smoked salmon pralines

TOASTS
Pre-heat the oven to 180 °C.

Place a sheet of baking paper or a baking mat on a baking tray.

Cut out 12 circles of puff pastry with a cutting ring of about 4-5 centimetres diameter.

Arrange on the baking tray and prick with a fork.

Bake for 7 to 8 minutes in the pre-heated oven.

Place on a wire rack to cool.

SMOKED SALMON
Soak the gelatine in cold water.

Mix the 100 grams of smoked salmon and 90 grams of fish fumet in a blender. Place in a mixing bowl.

Add the cream, the ketchup, the Tabasco and a few sprigs of dill. Season with pepper and salt and mix well.

Melt the squeezed gelatine over a low heat into the 35 grams of fish fumet.

Stir well through the salmon mixture and place in a piping bag.

Cover 12 little silicone moulds with a piece of smoked salmon. Fill further with the mousse.

Leave to stiffen in the freezer.

Arrange the toasts on a plate, remove the salmon mousse from the freezer and from the little moulds. Top each toast with a salmon mousse praline and finish with dill.

AGA

Place the baking tray on the bottom of the baking oven.

AGA: love at first sight!

As soon as I first saw an AGA and was allowed to cook on it, I was completely captivated. I even remember the date - 10 February 2004 - and the name of the chef with whom I followed an initiation course: Dirk Tanghe. Everything, but everything about this stove fitted in seamlessly with my way of cooking and the atmosphere that I like to create. The calm way of cooking. The spacious ovens in which you can prepare a full English breakfast in one go. The fact that you can bake directly on the large plates. I always say my house is built around my AGA and you can take that literally. My kitchen, in which my stove is central, is the throbbing heart of my home. In addition to the exceptional way of cooking, the AGA is also a source of cosiness and atmosphere. The children warm themselves at it when they come home in the winter, friends lean against it to enjoy the heat during our conversations. Yes, after all these years I'm even more convinced of my choice than I was at the beginning. My AGA and I: a never-ending love story!

Different parts of the AGA cooker

COOKING PLATES
The cooking plates have lids and offer enough space for 3 pots and pans at the same time.

BOILING PLATE or QUICK COOKING PLATE - 400 °C
Boiling liquids - stir-frying - roasting toast (famous AGA toast) - baking steak

SIMMERING PLATE - 250 ° C
Stewing and simmering - frying directly on the plate, e.g. eggs - heating milk

OVENS

The AGA cooker uses radiant heat that is emitted evenly and simultaneously from all sides by the cast iron ovens. This has a number of advantages. For example dishes sear quickly and there is little loss of moisture. In this way an optimal taste is retained and the vitamins remain in the products.

The temperature at the bottom of the oven is always slightly lower than in the middle or at the top, where it is hottest. That is why it is always indicated where in the oven the food should be placed. Always place a disk on a rack for optimal heat efficiency. Only pizzas can be baked directly on the bottom of the roasting oven.

Some AGA cookers have only two ovens, others have three or four. When an AGA has two ovens, the temperature is controlled largely by placing the dish higher or lower in the oven itself using the grid shelves supplied with the cooker. As an AGA owner, you will know that cooking with an AGA involves a degree of trial and error and that experience will teach you how high to place the dishes in the oven. If an AGA has only two ovens, the top oven will have a temperature of between 170 and 230°C, the lower one of between 100-120°C

WARMING OVEN (50 °C)
Warming up plates and dishes - leaving meat to cool - keeping food hot

SLOW COOKING OVEN (90 to 100 °C)
Slow cooking - stews, curries or meat dishes that require slow cooking - steaming root vegetables and rice

SIMMERING OVEN (120 °C)
Slow cooking - leg of lamb, stews, broth or stock, ragouts

BAKING OVEN (150 to 180 °C)
Baking light cakes, pies and biscuits - lasagna and dishes that require a lower temperature - baking bread

ROASTING OVEN (200 to 230 °C)
Roasting meat - baking at a high temperature - roasting poultry - grilling
The indirect radiant heat ensures perfect and even roast meat, with a rich taste and a crispy crust.

FOR 20 BLINIS

15 g fresh yeast
1.75 dl lukewarm water
1 teaspoon sugar
150 g flour
pinch of salt

1 egg yolk
1.75 dl milk
1 tablespoon soured cream
1 egg white
knob of softened butter

Blinis

Dissolve the yeast in the water and add the sugar. Allow to rest for a while.

Mix the flour with the salt. Add the egg yolks and the yeast mixture and beat into a batter.

Cover with a damp cloth and leave to rise for 1 hour.

Add the milk and the soured cream and mix.

Beat the egg white stiff and fold into the batter.

Open the lid of the simmering plate a few minutes beforehand.

Place a sheet of Bake-O-Glide on the simmering plate and brush with melted butter.

Using a small sauce spoon, spoon portions of dough onto the plate and form a blini about 4 to 5 centimetres across.

Cook for 1 minute and turn over with a palette knife. Cook for another 1 minute.

Place on a wire rack to cool.

TIP

Finish the blinis with salmon mousse (p. 319), smoked salmon and salmon eggs.

FOR 12 TULIPS

12 slices of white or brown bread, without crust
small knob of softened butter
fresh crab salad
shrimps
curly parsley

Bread tulips

Roll out the slices of bread thin with a rolling pin.

Push the bread slices into the buttered muffin moulds.

Brush the bread slices with melted butter.

Bake for 5 minutes until golden and crispy on the bottom of the roasting oven.

Leave to cool and fill with the crab salad and shrimps. Garnish with a tuft of parsley.

TIP

Fill the tulips with a filling of your choice.

TO SERVE 4
Consisting of:
- Egg fried on the simmering plate
- Merguez, mushrooms and tomatoes in the roasting oven
- Bacon on the grill plate in the roasting oven
- White beans in the roasting oven
- Toast in the toaster on the boiling plate

English breakfast

butter
4 eggs
pepper and salt

Egg fried on the simmering plate

Place a sheet of Bake-O-Glide on the simmering plate and brush with melted butter.

Break the eggs onto the plate and season with salt and pepper.

Close the lid. Check for doneness. After 2 minutes the eggs are ready.

Remove them from the plate with a palette knife.

AGA

Bake-O-Glide is a handy tool for mess-free baking on the plate itself. Fat is not necessary, but butter gives an extra flavour.

250 g Parisian mushrooms, cleaned and without stems
2 tomatoes, sliced
2 tablespoons olive oil
1 teaspoon oregano
4 merguez sausages

Merguez, mushrooms and tomatoes in the baking oven

Place the mushrooms and tomatoes in an aluminium baking tray and drizzle with olive oil. Sprinkle 1 teaspoon oregano over the tomatoes.

Place a grid on top and arrange the sausages on the grid.

Place the baking tray in the centre of the roasting oven and roast for 5 to 6 minutes.

4 slices of bacon

Bacon on the grill plate in the roasting oven

Place the bacon slices side by side on the grill plate.

Place the grill plate in a baking tray or on a rack right at the top of the roasting oven and grill for 7 to 8 minutes.

250 g white beans, dried
1.5 dl water
pepper and salt
2 sprigs savoury
20 cherry tomatoes
1 shallot, peeled and shredded
0.2 dl olive oil
10 g wheat flour
70 g tomato paste
1 tablespoon dried oregano

White beans in tomato sauce in the roasting oven

Rinse the beans and soak them overnight in water.

The next day, bring the beans to the boil on the boiling plate with the soaking water, a pinch of salt and the savoury. Cover with the lid and cook for 1 hour in the slow cooking oven.

Drain the beans and collect the cooking liquid. Put the beans into an oven dish.

Purée the cherry tomatoes.

Sauté the shallot on the boiling plate in the olive oil. Sprinkle the flour over the shallot and stir well. Moisten the beans with 350 grams of cooking liquid and stir with a whisk.

Add the mixed cherry tomatoes, tomato purée and oregano and season with salt and pepper.

Let the sauce cook for another 5 minutes on the boiling plate and stir into a smooth sauce.

Pour the sauce over the beans in the oven dish and keep hot in the warming oven.

4 slices of bread, without crust and spread with melted butter

Toast in the toaster on the boiling plate

Pre-heat the toaster briefly on the boiling plate under the closed lid.

Clamp the slices of bread inside the toaster.

Place the toaster on the boiling plate and close the lid. Open the lid after 1 minute and turn the toaster over. Toast for another minute under the closed lid.

Remove the toaster from the plate and remove the toast. Keep the toast hot in the warming oven.

TIP

The toaster is pre-heated on the boiling plate to prevent the toast from sticking to the toaster.

30 chillies

Dried chillies

CHILLI NECKLACE

Thread the chillies onto a string using a needle. Stick the needle in the thickest part of the stem just above the fruit.

Hang the chilli necklace over the warming plate for a few days until dry.

CHILLI POWDER

Place a sheet of baking paper or a baking mat on a baking tray.

Place the dried chillies on the baking tray and dry for 3 hours in the slow cooking oven.

Remove the stems with the string and mix to a powder.

TIP

A necklace of dried chillies is very decorative in the kitchen.
Chilli powder keeps well in a closed jar.
Careful with your eyes when mixing the chillies.

2 oranges

Dried orange slices

Wash the oranges well and pat them dry.

Cut the oranges into 3-millimetre slices with a mandolin slicer.

Place a sheet of baking paper or a baking mat on a baking tray.

Spread the slices over the oven tray.

Leave to dry for 3 hours in in the slow cooking oven.

Remove from the oven and leave to cool.

TIP

Use the dried orange slices as decoration in a cocktail.

FOR 4 TYPES OF VEGETABLE CHIPS

1 fresh beetroot, unpeeled
1 sweet potato, unpeeled
2 large carrots, peeled
6 waxy potatoes, unpeeled
2 tablespoons sunflower oil
olive oil
1 teaspoon flake salt

Vegetable chips

Wash the vegetables under cold running water and dry.

Cut the vegetables into wafer-thin slices with a mandolin and mix each time with 1/2 tablespoon sunflower oil.

Place the vegetable slices separately in a single layer on a wire rack.

Brush the vegetable slices with olive oil.

Place the grid for 90 minutes to 2 hours in the slow cooking oven. You can place several grids on top of each other. Turn the chips after 45 minutes to dry all sides.

Remove the chips from the grid and leave for a while on kitchen paper and sprinkle with flaky salt.

Leave to cool.

TIP

Respect the amount of oil so that the chips can dry crispy.
Also sprinkle the chips with paprika or a spice of your choice.

FOR 20 PANCAKES
100 g self-raising flour
1 egg
150 g whole milk
handful of green herbs (basil, flat parsley and mint)
sunflower oil
extra green herbs for garnish
1 tub of Philadelphia with herbs

Herb pancakes

Open the lid of the simmering plate a few minutes beforehand.

Mix the self-raising flour, egg, whole milk and green herbs into a dough in a blender.

Place a sheet of Bake-O-Glide on the simmering plate and brush with a little sunflower oil.

Spoon the dough onto the plate with a sauce spoon and bake for 1 minute. Turn the pancakes over and bake for another minute.

Remove the pancakes from the plate and keep hot on a rack in the warming oven.

Place eight pancakes on top of each other and spread a layer of Philadelphia between each. Garnish with additional green herbs.

FOR 4 JARS
800 g oranges
1000 g sugar
pulp of 1 mango, diced
pulp of 2 passion fruits
2 tablespoons lemon juice
2 tablespoons water

Orange, mango and passion fruit marmalade

Wash the peel of the oranges thoroughly under hot water.

Bring the oranges to the boil in plenty of water on the boiling plate.

Cover with a lid and simmer for 2 hours in the cooking or simmering oven.

Drain the oranges and leave to dry.

Cut the oranges into thin slices and chop finely.

Mix the orange, sugar, mango, passion fruit, lemon juice and water and bring to the boil on the boiling plate. Stir to dissolve the sugar.

Move the bowl to the simmering plate and reduce to marmalade for 20 minutes. Stir regularly.

Distribute the marmalade between the jars and close each jar with a lid. Turn the pots upside down to cool.

FOR A Ø 25 CM TURBAN CAKE MOULD

FOR THE CAKE
250 g butter, at room temperature
75 g granulated sugar
75 g light brown caster sugar
zest of 1 orange
zest of 1 lime
4 eggs
150 g marmalade
225 g self-raising flour

DECORATION
3 dl water
200 g sugar
2 oranges, finely sliced
1 passion fruit
mint leaves

Marmalade cake

CAKE

Beat the butter, granulated sugar and caster sugar in a food processor with a beater.

Add the orange and lime zest and mix well.

Leave the food processor running and add the eggs one by one. Add half the marmalade.

Gradually add the flour and mix until smooth.

Place a silicone turban mould onto a baking tray and spoon the mixture into it. Smooth with a palette knife.

Place the baking tray on a rack in the centre of the baking oven and bake for 45 minutes.

Remove the cake from the oven and leave to cool.

DECORATION

Put the other half of the marmalade in a pan and place it somewhere on the corner of the boiling plate so that it can melt slowly.

Bring the water and the sugar to the boil on the boiling plate. Add the orange slices and move the pan to the slow cooking oven. Candy for 30 minutes and drain.

Remove from the mould and place on a tray. Brush the top of the cake with the melted marmalade and top with the slices of candied orange. Finish with the passion fruit and mint leaves.

TIP

Make some more candied orange slices, drain well and dry. Place a sheet of baking paper or a baking mat on a baking tray and arrange the slices on it. Place the baking tray in the slow cooking oven for 45 minutes for delicious dried orange slices.

FOR 1 SERVING
1 handful of well-rinsed mussels
½ blade of celery, cleaned and sliced
6 flat parsley leaves
0.5 dl white wine
curry powder
sprig of thyme
½ spring onion

Mussels

Place all ingredients in a shallow aluminium dish.

Place this directly onto the boiling plate and close the lid.

Cook the mussels for 3 minutes until all shells are open.

TIP

This simple recipe is ideal if you need a few mussels as a garnish.

TO SERVE 2

FOR THE MUSSELS
600 g mussels, cleaned
1 onion, peeled and roughly chopped
2 celery stalks, cleaned and roughly chopped

FOR THE SAUCE
1 carrot, cleaned and diced
1 leek, cleaned and finely sliced
1 onion, peeled and shredded
8 cloves garlic, peeled and shredded
4 tablespoons olive oil
0.6 dl Ricard
4 tablespoons dried tarragon
1 tablespoon ketchup
2.5 dl cream 40%
8 saffron threads
pepper and salt
2 tomatoes, peeled, seeded and diced
20 chives, finely chopped

Mussels with fine spices

MUSSELS
Cook the mussels with the onion and celery on the boiling plate under the lid and shake regularly until the shells open.

Drain the mussels and collect the cooking liquid. Reserve.

SAUCE
Fry the carrot, leek and onion in the olive oil on the boiling plate.

Deglaze with the Ricard and leave to simmer for a while.

Add the mussel liquid, tarragon, ketchup, cream and saffron and season with salt and pepper.

Reduce.

Strain the sauce.

Spoon the mussels into a bowl, pour the sauce over it, add the diced tomato and sprinkle with the chives.

FOR 2 FLATBREADS
FOR THE DOUGH
200 g wheat flour
5 g baking powder
150 g Greek yoghurt
pinch of salt

1 clove garlic, peeled and pressed
1 teaspoon ras el hanout
1 teaspoon olive oil

AND ALSO
40 g butter, melted
2 sprigs rosemary
pinch of flake salt

Naan flatbread

Mix all the ingredients in a food processor with a dough hook and knead for 3 minutes to a supple dough.

Divide the dough in half and roll out each portion into an oval on a floured work surface.

Open the toaster.

Place an oval piece of dough on one side, brush with the melted butter, put a sprig of rosemary on top and season with flake salt.

Close the toaster and place it directly onto the boiling plate.

Close the lid and bake for 3 minutes.

Open the lid, turn the toaster over and bake again for 3 minutes with the lid closed.

FOR 20 PANCAKES

100 g self-raising flour

25 g sugar

1 egg

150 g whole milk

10 g vanilla sugar

Pancakes

Open the lid of the simmering plate a few minutes beforehand.

Mix all ingredients into a smooth batter.

Place a sheet of Bake-O-Glide onto the simmering plate. Smear the sheet with sunflower oil.

Spoon a sauce spoon of batter onto the plate.

Bake for one minute and flip the pancake when the topside is dry. Bake for another minute. Three pancakes fit on the plate.

Keep the pancakes hot on a rack in the warming oven.

Stack eight pancakes on top of each other and finish as desired.

FOR 4 PORTIONS
2 dl corn oil or sunflower oil
125 g popping corn
50 g of sugar

Popcorn

IN A PAN
Heat a cast iron pan with lid in the slow cooking oven until nice and hot.

Place the pan on the boiling plate and heat the oil.

Add the corn in a quick movement and cover with the lid.

Shake regularly so that the bottom grains do not burn.

Open the lid only when you no longer hear popping noises.

Place the popcorn in a bowl and sprinkle with sugar or salt.

DIRECTLY ON THE BOILING PLATE
Place a sheet of Bake-O-Glide onto the boiling plate.

Spread a layer of corn onto the plate, keeping 3 centimetres away from the edge.

Close the lid quickly and open it again only when you no longer hear popping noises.

Place the popcorn in a bowl and sprinkle with sugar or salt.

TIP

With maple syrup: heat a little maple syrup and stir in the popcorn. Keep stirring so that the popcorn doesn't stick together.
With Italian herbs: mix dried Italian herbs with pepper, salt and ½ teaspoon garlic powder. Sprinkle over the popcorn and shake well.
Replace the Italian herbs with paprika powder, curry powder or ras el hanout.

FOR 2 WRAPS

100 g soured cream
10 sprigs chives, finely chopped
pepper and salt
2 wraps
2 slices of smoked salmon
150 g cheddar, grated

Salmon wraps

Mix the soured cream with the chives and season with salt and pepper. Store in the refrigerator.

Open the toaster.

Put a wrap on one side. Top with the smoked salmon and cheddar and put a second wrap on top.

Close the toaster and place it directly onto the boiling plate.

Close the lid and bake for 2 minutes.

Open the lid, flip the toaster over and bake for 1 minutes with the lid closed.

Remove the wraps from the toaster and cut into triangles.

Serve with the soured cream.

TIP

Replace the smoked salmon with chorizo.

Recipe index

A

Almond cake with pear *202*
Almond snaps ('chatterboxes') *226*
Amaretti *203*
Apple pie *206*
Apple strudel *200*
Applesauce tart *204*

B

Bacon on the grill plate in the roasting oven *328*
Banana bread *248*
Basic dough for pizza *88*
Basic recipe puff pastry *309*
Basic tomato sauce *269*
Bean dish *74*
Belgian endive dish with minced meat *181*
Biscuit rose *205*
Bisque d'homard *27*
Blanquette of veal *156*
Blinis *322*
Blueberry cake *208*
Boeuf bourguignon *152*
Bread tulips *324*
Breakfast pistolets *249*
Brioche oven dish with dulce de leche *250*
Brownies *209*
Burned pear tart *310*
Burrata with roasted aubergine *75*
Buttermilk stampers *67*
Butternut with kale stuffing *72*

C

Camembert fondue *15*
Canard à l'orange *128*
Cannelloni *36*
Cassoulet *131*
Cauliflower snacks *14*
Celery gratin Anne-Marie *283*
Champagne risotto with ricotta *47*
Cheese and bacon pizza *293*
Cheese biscuits *313*
Cherry flan *222*
Chicken balls in Flanders fields *303*
Chicken cream soup with leek *29*
Chocolate bars *214*
Chocolate cake with hazelnut *213*
Chocolate cookie with hazelnut *220*
Chocolate-tipped meringue sticks (billygoat hoofs) *210*
Christmas cake *225*
Cinnamon sprites *224*
Cocoa biscuits *212*
Coconut bar *227*
Coconut rocks *232*
Cod boulangère *300*
Coq au vin *132*
Cottage pie *78*
Crème caramel *195*
Crostini with avocado *16*
Crusty vol-au-vent *147*

D

Dorade with ratatouille and pesto *104*
Dried chillies *330*
Dried orange slices *330*
Duchesse potatoes with parsnips *66*
Dundee cake *218*

E

Egg fried on the simmering plate *327*
English breakfast *325*

F

Farm chicken crapaudine *285*
Fast bread pudding *241*
Fish soup with pastis *33*

Fish waterzooi *120*
Flatbread with avocado spread *257*
Fondant potatoes *59*
Frangipane cake *215*
Frittata with cauliflower *49*

G

Gingerbread *233*
Gingerbread crumble with apple and pear *196*
Glazed belly ribs *173*
Glazed cod *105*
Glazed duck *139*
Grape bread *254*
Gratinated potato puree with sausages *60*
Guinea fowl with morels *143*

H

Haddock rarebit with white cabbage and kale *116*
Hare paté *182*
Hare stew *186*
Hasselback potatoes with bay leaves *65*
Herb pancakes *332*
Honey biscuits *221*

I

Involtini di pesce *270*
Italian minced meat dish *174*

K

Kilometre tart with fresh fruit *314*
Kohlrabi gratin *81*

L

Lamb daube *163*
Lamb tagine *294*

Lasagne quattro formaggi *39*
Lasagne with salmon and fennel *38*
Leek rolls *84*
Leg of lamb with figs *160*
Lemon sand cake *217*
Lemon sole with turmeric *119*
Lobster scarmoza *106*
Lobster with green herbs *111*
Luxury bread with sweet cinnamon filling *258*

M

Marmalade cake *334*
"Marieke's cups"- yoghurt tart *297*
Meat and vegetable confetti *286*
Meatballs with pumpkin and oyster mushrooms *168*
Meatloaf *178*
Mediterranean meat loaf *307*
Merguez, mushrooms and tomatoes in the baking oven *328*
Meringue with fresh cranberries *192*
Mexican vegetable dish *82*
Minced bread with hidden eggs *170*
Minestrone *30*
Misérable *228*
Morrocan bread *260*
Moussaka *165*
Mushroom strudel with spinach *77*
Mussels *336*
Mussels thermidor *289*
Mussels with fine spices *337*
Mussels with leek *109*

N

Naan flatbread *338*
Nut cake with salted caramel *231*
Nut rolls *261*

O

Orange tart with liqueur *242*
Orange, mango and passion fruit marmalade *333*
Ossobuco *159*
Oven dish à la Delphine Parmentier *290*
Oven fries with chilli mayonnaise *53*

P

Pancakes *339*
Parmentier with shrimps *68*
Pasta pomodoro with lobster in basil butter *275*
Pasta shells with kale and artichoke *44*
Pasta with merguez *43*
Paté with pistachios *176*
Pea soup with smoked sausage *28*
Pear and roquefort bread *263*
Pear frangipane *299*
Pear tart with almonds *234*
Pesto roll *253*
Pheasant stew *146*
Pigeon with peas *135*
Pizza pancetta *91*
Pizza raclette *91*
Pizza with broccoli and spinach *89*
Pizza with ceps and quail egg *88*
Plaice with clams *113*
Plaice with red endive *112*
Popcorn *340*
Potato dish with mozzarella *58*
Potato gratin *55*
Potato pie *52*
Potato soup with rosemary crackers *24*
Potatoes with fungi, sage and bacon *54*
Potatoes with tomato crust *57*
Pumpkin lasagna *40*

Q

Quatre-quarts apple cake *236*
Quatre-quarts cake *235*
Quatre-quartsgingerbread-apple cake *236*

R

Rabbit as mum makes it *185*
Radiatori al 4 formaggi *276*
Radicchio with ricotta *85*
Red fruit with quark *197*
Redfish with tomato and asparagus *114*
Rice tart express *240*
Rice tart with coconut *239*
Roast belly pork *171*
Roast pheasant *136*
Roast potatoes *61*
Roast sweet potatoes with chicken *62*
Roasted cauliflower *79*
Roasted pumpkin *80*
Roasted veal crown *155*

S

Saddle of lamb with herb crust *161*
Salmon wraps *341*
Sausage rolls *179*
Scones with cheese, olives and onion *19*
Sea bass with aioli *123*
Slow-cooked leg of lamb with mint *166*
Smoked sardines *110*
Snails with herb butter *17*
Sole à la dugléré *115*
Sole hollandaise *124*
Soufflé with green herbs *21*
Spaghetti with sage butter *279*
Spring chickens Brabançonne *304*
Spring chickens with wild mushroom cream sauce *144*
Stuffed cauliflower *175*

Stuffed pheasant *140*
Sugar loaf *264*
Swedish meatballs *149*

T

Tagliatelle with ricotta and pancetta *280*
Tartine russe *245*
Toast in the toaster on the boiling plate *329*
Toasts with smoked salmon pralines *319*
Tray bake with chicken and paprika *95*
Tray bake with salmon, carrot and bok choy *96*
Tray bake with sweet potato, fennel and ricotta *99*
Tray bake with young carrots and chipolatas *94*
Turkey ossobuco *273*

V

Vegetable chips *331*

W

White beans in tomato sauce in the roasting oven *329*
Wolffish with curry *125*

Y

Young venison ragout *189*

Z

Za'atar rolls *265*

Ingredient index

A

almond extract *202, 225, 228*
almond flour *200, 234, 242*
almond, ground *202, 206, 208, 210, 215, 220, 228, 240, 299*
almonds *214, 218, 234*
amaretto *218*
anchovy *14*
Anne-Marie farm cheese *283*
apple syrup *203*
apples *125, 146, 196, 204, 206, 208, 236, 297*
apricot jam *206, 210, 217, 218, 227, 236, 310*
artichoke *44, 123*
asparagus *94, 114*
aubergine *75*
avocado *16, 257*

B

bacon *49, 54, 58, 131, 132, 136, 152, 171, 176, 182, 293, 304, 328*
bananas *248*
basil *104, 275*
beans *30, 74, 82, 96, 131, 329*
beef *152, 168*
beer *185, 289*
beetroot *331*
Belgian endive *181, 304*
berries, blue *208, 228, 314*
berries, red *197, 314*
blackberries *314*
bleu d'auvergne *39*
bok choy *96, 307*
brazil nuts *231*
bread *67, 140, 143, 241, 249, 325*
breadcrumbs *60, 78, 149, 168, 170, 178, 179, 270, 290*
broccoli *30, 89*
broccolini *94*
Brussels sprouts *303*
burrata *75*
butter *17, 124, 166, 245, 275*
buttermilk *67, 84*

C

calvados *236*
camembert *15, 174*
candy sugar *226*
cannelloni *36*
capers *14*
carrots *27, 29, 30, 33, 65, 94, 96, 120, 132, 152, 156, 159, 163, 165, 168, 185, 189, 273, 279, 285, 286, 290, 294, 303, 331, 337*
cashews *104*
cauliflower *49, 79, 175*
cauliflower rice *14*
celery *27, 28, 29, 30, 33, 109, 119, 120, 149, 159, 165, 174, 273, 289, 336, 337*
cep *88*
champagne *47*
chanterelle mushrooms *88*
cheddar *14, 19, 39, 72, 175, 241*
cheese *14, 15, 16, 19, 21, 36, 38, 39, 40, 43, 44, 47, 55, 58, 62, 72, 75, 78, 81, 85, 88, 89, 91, 94, 99, 104, 106, 109, 140, 165, 174, 175, 181, 192, 228, 241, 249, 253, 257, 263, 270, 276, 280, 283, 289, 293, 297, 313, 332*
cherries *222*
cherry tomatoes *49, 74, 95, 104, 168, 279, 307, 329*
chervil *21*
chestnuts *140*
chicken *62, 95, 132, 143, 147, 285, 303*
chicken liver *176*
chickpeas *78*
chilli flakes *37, 119*
chillies *62, 105, 330*
chimichurri *175*
chipolota *94, 143*
chives *17, 21*
chocolate *186, 209, 210, 212, 214, 220, 242, 299*
chocolate chips *220, 228*
chorizo *40*
ciabatta *16*
cinnamon *224, 258*
clams *33, 113*
cocoa powder *212, 213*
coconut milk *125, 239*
cod *105, 300*
cognac *27, 135, 136, 140, 149, 176*
comté cheese *88, 293*
corn *82, 340*
courgette *30, 36, 38, 104, 123, 165, 286, 307*
couscous *286*

crab salad *325*
cranberries *136, 149, 192, 225*
cranberry jam *139*
crayfish *47, 120*
cream *21, 24, 27, 29, 39, 49, 54, 55, 68, 81, 109, 116, 119, 120, 135, 136, 140, 144, 146, 149, 156, 196, 214, 228, 231, 241, 242, 276, 280, 289, 310, 319, 337*
crème patisserie *310, 314*
croutons *113*
cucumber *77*
curry powder *125*

D
deer calf *189*
dessert rice *239, 240*
dorade *104*
duck *128, 131, 139*
duck liver *143*

E
egg *49, 53, 67, 88, 123, 124, 140, 166, 170, 192, 195, 327*
emmentaler *78, 181*

F
fennel *33, 38, 99, 123, 279, 300*
feta *94*
fig jam *140*
figs *85, 160, 228*
filo pastry *77*
fish *33, 38, 96, 104, 105, 112, 113, 114, 115, 116, 119, 120, 123, 124, 125, 241, 270, 300, 319*
fish fumet *33, 109, 111, 115, 119, 120, 125, 319*
flaked almonds *202, 209, 210, 225, 226, 234, 236, 299, 310*
foie gras *140*
forest mushrooms *144*
fungi *54*

G
garlic *17, 123, 159*
gilt-head bream *33*
gin *197*
ginger powder *233*
gingerbread *186, 196, 236*

gingerbread spices *203, 233*
goat cheese *62, 104*
gorgonzola *276*
Grand Marnier *128*
grapes *254*
grappa *270*
grated coconut *227*
Greek yoghurt *77, 225, 338*
ground coconut *232*
gruyère *21, 38, 55, 109, 249, 289, 313*
guinea fowl *143*

H
haddock *116*
ham *143, 170, 249, 283*
hare *182, 186*
hazelnut flour *213*
hazelnut powder *220*
hazelnuts *104*
Hendrik Geeraert beer *289*
herb cheese *72*
honey *221*

J
jalapeño *82*
jam *206, 210, 217, 218, 227, 236, 297, 310*

K
kale *44, 72, 116*
ketchup *112, 170, 319, 337*
kohlrabi *81, 286*

L
lamb *160, 161, 163, 165, 166, 294*
lamb's lettuce *285*
lasagne sheets *38, 39*
leek *28, 29, 30, 33, 68, 84, 109, 120, 156, 293, 303, 337*
lemon *124, 159, 217, 300*
lemon sole *119*
lentils *72*
Liège syrup *146, 233*
lime *104, 125, 136, 161, 192, 239, 334*
lobster *27, 106, 111, 275*

M
Madeira *143*
Malines chicken *29*
mango *333*
marmalade *334*
Marsala *202*
marzipan *225*
mashed potatoes *78, 290*
merguez sausage *43, 294, 328*
minced meat *36, 143, 147, 149, 156, 165, 168, 170, 174, 175, 178, 179, 181, 286, 290, 303, 307*
mint *166*
mixed spices *225*
morels *143*
mozzarella *38, 39, 58, 89, 91, 165, 253, 270, 276, 279*
mushrooms *40, 77, 95, 99, 132, 146, 147, 152, 156, 174, 303, 328*
mussels *33, 109, 120, 289, 336, 337*

N
Noilly Prat *119, 144*
nuts *14, 85, 104, 140, 143, 231, 261, 313*

O
Old Bruges *91*
olives *19, 95, 123*
onion *19*
orange *94, 112, 128, 149, 159, 242, 330, 333, 334*
oyster mushroom *168*

P
pancetta *62, 91, 280*
panko breadcrumbs *161*
Parmesan cheese *21, 24, 30, 43, 44, 47, 52, 54, 77, 84, 85, 116, 165, 178, 273*
parsley *17, 21, 29, 44, 132, 140, 143, 147, 156, 159, 161, 170, 178, 182, 270, 273, 289, 294, 303, 336*
parsnip *39, 66, 146*
passata *30, 88, 89, 91, 159, 165, 269, 280, 286, 307*
passion fruit *334*
pasta *30, 43, 44*
pastis *33*
Patrelle aroma *146*
pearl onions *132, 144, 156*

pears *196, 202, 234, 263, 299, 310*
peas *28, 30, 135*
pecorino *39, 40, 165*
pepper, sweet, pointed *36, 77, 78, 82, 95, 104, 119, 175, 294, 307*
pesto *89, 253, 260*
pheasant *136, 140, 146*
Philadelpia *332*
pigeon *135*
pine nuts *44, 116*
pineapple *314*
pistachio nuts *143, 176*
pizza base *88, 89, 91*
plaice *33, 112, 113*
pointed cabbage *294*
pork *168, 170, 171, 173, 174, 175, 176, 178, 181, 182, 286*
pork liver *182*
port *140, 159, 189*
potatoes *24, 52, 53, 54, 55, 57, 58, 59, 60, 61, 62, 65, 66, 67, 68, 94, 163, 165, 174, 283, 285, 300, 304, 331*
processed cheese *276*
puff pastry *52, 147, 179, 200, 204, 214, 222, 239, 309, 310, 313, 314, 319*
pumpkin *30, 40, 72, 80, 168, 189, 279*
pumpkin seeds *279*

G
quark *197*
quorn *82*

R
rabbit *185*
raclette cheese *91*
radicchio *85*
raisins *200, 204, 218*
raspberries *197, 228, 314*
red endive *112*
redfish *114*
Reypenaer *36*
Ricard *173, 337*
rice *47*
ricotta *16, 36, 40, 43, 44, 47, 85, 99, 257, 280*
Rodenbach *185*
Roquefort *81, 263*

roquette *47*
rosemary *24*
rum *200, 204*

S
saffron *123, 240*
sage *54, 279*
salad *77, 249*
salmon *38, 96, 120, 319, 241*
sambal *106*
sardines *110, 270*
sausage *28, 40, 43, 60, 94, 131, 178, 294, 328*
scarmoza *106*
sea bass *123*
semolina *222*
shallot *17*
sherry *29, 124, 146*
shortcrust pastry *297*
shrimps *67, 68, 313, 325*
snails *17*
sole *33, 115, 120, 124*
soured cream *52, 65, 293, 324, 241*
soy sauce *128*
spaghetti *275, 279*
spelt flour *263*
spice mix *149, 332*
spinach *36, 77, 78, 81, 89, 96, 168*
spring chicken *144, 304*
stock *156, 273, 286, 294, 303, 304*
stock, fish *38, 68*
stock, game *136, 146, 186*
stock, lamb *163*
stock, poultry *128, 135, 139, 147, 168, 304*
stock, veal *143, 144, 149, 152, 159, 176, 189, 307*
strawberries *197, 314*
sugar *192, 195, 231, 264*
sweet potato *99, 331*
sweet soy sauce (ketjap) *139, 171, 179*

T
taco sauce *82*
tagliatelle *280*
tahini *77*
Taleggio *276*
tarragon *21*
tomato ketchup *74, 170*
tomato paste *27, 30, 33, 106, 131, 163, 165, 173, 174, 273, 329*
tomato pulp *168*
tomatoes *16, 27, 30, 36, 40, 57, 75, 78, 106, 112, 113, 114, 115, 131, 159, 163, 257, 269, 273, 276, 280, 328, 337*
tomatoes, sun-dried *43, 91, 113, 275*
tortilla chips *82*
turkey *273*
turmeric *119*
turnip *146, 294, 303*

V
vanilla ice cream *299*
veal *155, 156, 159, 174, 181, 286, 307*
vegan cheese *82*

W
walnuts *85, 313*
whisky *15, 242*
white cabbage *30, 116*
white raddish *286*
wine, red *132, 152, 163, 165, 174, 182, 186*
wine, white *29, 33, 36, 39, 43, 74, 77, 106, 109, 111, 113, 115, 116, 120, 131, 168, 263, 336*
wolffish *125*
wraps *241*

Y
yacón *303*
yoghurt *297*

Thanks to:
Mi Casa - micasa.be
Scapa Home - www.scapahome.com

COLOPHON

www.lannoo.com
Register on our website and we will send you a regular newsletter with information about new books and with interesting, exclusive offers

Text: Claudia Allemeersch
Final editing: Edward Vanhoutte
English translation: Michael Lomax
Photography: Heikki Verdurme
Graphic design: Best Advice

If you have any comments or questions, please contact our editorial team at:
redactielifestyle@lannoo.com

© Lannoo Publishers, Tielt, 2021
D/2021/45/407 - NUR 440
ISBN: 9789401479271

All rights reserved. No part of this publication may be reproduced, stored in an automated database and/or published in any form or in any way, whether electronically, mechanically or in any other way without prior permission in writing from the publishers.